P9-AQH-511

SLAVERY AS A CAUSE OF THE CIVIL WAR

Problems in American Civilization

PREPARED UNDER THE EDITORSHIP OF

Earl Latham

George Rogers Taylor

George F. Whicher

1 The Declaration of Independence and the Constitution
2 The Turner Thesis concerning the Role of the Frontier in American History
3 Jackson versus Biddle – The Struggle over the Second Bank of the United States
4 The Transcendentalist Revolt against Materialism
5 Slavery as a Cause of the Civil War
6 Democracy and the Gospel of Wealth
7 John D. Rockefeller – Robber Baron or Industrial Statesman?
8 The New Deal – Revolution or Evolution?

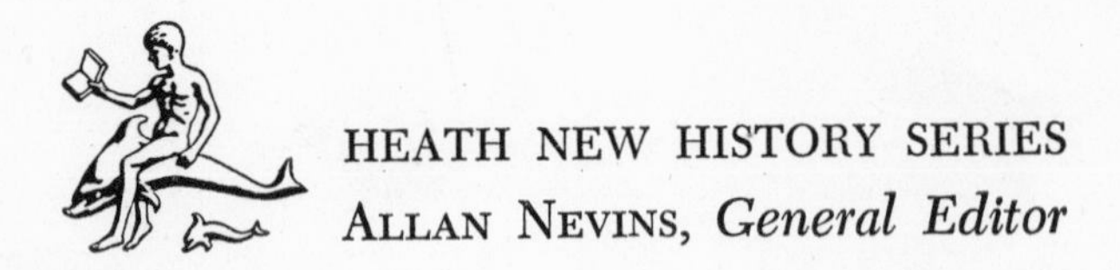

HEATH NEW HISTORY SERIES
ALLAN NEVINS, *General Editor*

Slavery as a Cause of the Civil War

EDITED WITH AN INTRODUCTION BY

Edwin C. Rozwenc

Problems in American Civilization

READINGS SELECTED BY THE
DEPARTMENT OF AMERICAN STUDIES
AMHERST COLLEGE

D. C. HEATH AND COMPANY: Boston

PRINTED IN THE UNITED STATES OF AMERICA

Offices

Boston New York Chicago Dallas
Atlanta San Francisco London

INTRODUCTION

THE reason for the fascination exerted upon most Americans by the Civil War is not hard to discover, for the conflict of sections was a highly dramatic crisis in our historical development. Deadly combat between two sections of the same nation, between cousins and even brothers, is the kind of tragic theme out of which legends naturally spring. Its imaginative appeal has been well described by Henry Seidel Canby:

> Our Civil War is dramatic with a sharp and simple theme – karma: destiny as determined by irrevocable acts, a conflict of two civilizations bound together like twin enemies in a trap of their own making, the heavy payment of innocent men for the will of their ancestors, the fierce struggle of moral codes unlike though resemblant, the cruel consequence of an impersonal economics pouring like a rock slide over happy valleys.[1]

And so American poets and novelists in great numbers have sought to exploit the rich possibilities of this fateful period. Aside from men like Walt Whitman, James Russell Lowell, and William Cullen Bryant, who were writing in the midst of the conflict, such notable contributors to our literary tradition as Joel Chandler Harris, George W. Cable, Stephen Crane, Vachel Lindsay, Edwin Markham, Carl Sandburg, Stephen Vincent Benét, and William Faulkner have made use of Civil War themes. In addition, a staggering amount of popular fiction, both novels and short stories, dealing with the Civil War has been consumed in the last fifty years by an eager reading public. All of these efforts have been fed by a never-ending stream of published memoirs and diaries of officers and soldiers who had worn either the "blue" or the "gray." The present-day acceptance of the epic nature of the conflict is reflected in the title of a recently published anthology of reminiscences and eyewitness accounts of Civil War battles, *The American Iliad.*

For historians, the Civil War has further implications. The conflict marked a bloody dividing line across American history, indicating a crucial stage in the transition from an agricultural, rural, religious, and personalized America to an industrial, urban, secular, and institutionalized America. This pivotal significance has made it a basic factor in practically every attempt since 1865 to develop a meaningful interpretation of American history. No doubt it also helps to account for the divergences of such interpretations, for most human crises of great magnitude and complexity in world history offer different meanings to different men at different times, and the Civil War was such a crisis.

Conflicting opinions have given rise to a whole series of "problems" about the Civil War. One of these, and really the first question one has to ask, is what

[1] Introduction to Stephen Vincent Benét, *John Brown's Body* (New York, Rinehart and Company, Inc., 1941), p. viii.

caused the Civil War? Why did Americans who lived south of the Potomac and Ohio rivers think that they had to fight Americans who lived north of those rivers? The efforts of historians, both amateur and professional, to answer that question have produced a growing number of academic battles and skirmishes in which books and articles and sharp sallies in the meetings of professional societies have replaced shot and shell and bayonet.

The signing of the articles of surrender by General Lee at Appomattox ended the military conflict, but it was the signal for the beginning of a cold war of sectional apologetics, carried on in the writings of northerners and southerners in the first generation after the war. During this period sectional bitterness and personal feelings of hatred were still so deep as to encourage wide acceptance of a kind of "devil theory" concerning the cause of the war. Northern writers insisted that the full guilt for the four years of bloodshed must be laid upon a group of conspiratorial slaveholders who were determined to rule or ruin the Union. These southern "fire-eaters," it was held, had been the aggressors by preferring secession to compromise in 1860–1861, by seizing federal property, and by firing on Fort Sumter. Southern writers, on the contrary, insisted that the cloven hoof was really on the other foot. They assigned the major responsibility for the war to "fanatical" abolitionists and "Black" Republicans, whose evil purpose toward the South and the Union had been finally revealed in John Brown's raid and the ensuing elevation of John Brown to the status of a martyr in much northern opinion.

These oversimplified explanations tended to disappear when a new generation of historians, less partisan and less emotional, appeared at the end of the century. In any case, the "devil theory" cannot stand up in the face of modern historical scholarship, particularly in the face of the general implications of such an essay as Charles A. Beard's "The Devil Theory of War." Yet in the last two decades a subtler and more sophisticated kind of "devil theory" has grown up, expressed in the writings of the "repressible conflict" school of historians and represented in our readings by the selection from J. G. Randall, one of its leading exponents. In this interpretation, psychological factors, such as sectional pride and honor, fanaticism, reformers' zeal, and religious enthusiasm, are emphasized. Behind the mounting hysteria, it is charged, were agitators on both sides, who served up the devil's brew of misunderstanding, hatred, and fear which prevented a rational solution of the issues of the day. This fanatical agitation of small groups on both sides is regarded as the central dynamic which caused an unnecessary war.

Another debate over the causes of the Civil War which emerged in the years immediately after the conflict turned on the question of constitutional theory. As a matter of fact, the constitutional controversy became a favorite game for southern leaders of the "lost cause," notably Jefferson Davis and Alexander H. Stephens, the former president and vice-president of the Confederacy. Stephens, for example, pictured the "lost cause" as not merely the cause of the South but of the whole Union as it was meant to be by the states which had formed it. Beside this noble and unselfish ideal, the "whole subject of slavery . . . was, to the Seceding States, but a drop in the ocean." The most vigorous northern answer was made by John W. Burgess, who characterized the southern constitutional arguments as "sophistries based upon confused premises" and dismissed as contrary to "sound political science" the effort to make secession appear to be a legal action and not rebellion. In our own day the long and involved constitutional studies of Stephens and Burgess can be safely allowed to gather dust on the shelves, for Arthur M. Schlesinger's devastating essay entitled "The States Rights Fetish" has made it impossible for any self-respecting historian to accept the states' rights issue as a fundamental cause of the Civil War.

Only one of the earliest explanations of the cause of the Civil War has continued to have any respectability among twentieth century scholars. That is the position taken by most of the earlier northern writers that slavery was the primary cause of the Civil War. The first formulation of the slavery thesis was expressed in ethical terms, picturing the Civil War as an "irrepressible" moral conflict between freedom and slavery. First the abolitionists and then more moderate men in the North, it was said, had become aroused over an institution which seemed to them to be contrary to the laws of God and Nature and to the principles of American democracy. The political agitation over fugitive slaves and the territories, the preachments of northern clergymen, and the influence of *Uncle Tom's Cabin* created in them a determination to prevent the extension of slavery and ultimately to cleanse the national conscience by destroying slavery where it already existed. The southern defense of slavery as a positive good, supported by scriptural quotations, brought the issue to an irreconcilable moral division of the two sections, and war became inevitable. This view is represented in the readings by an excerpt from the work of James F. Rhodes, one of the classic American historians of the end of the nineteenth century.

In our own generation, many historians continue to hold to the primacy of the slavery issue in causing the Civil War, but in general the emphasis has shifted from the moral terms in which Rhodes defined the issue to its political, social, and economic aspects. The essays by Ulrich B. Phillips, Russel B. Nye, and Bernard DeVoto which are reprinted in this book are samples of the varying interpretations of the way in which the slavery issue actually operated to produce ultimate war.

The remarkable growth of the economic interpretation of history during the twentieth century has had its impact on interpretations of the Civil War. Although there were others before them, it was Charles A. Beard and Mary R. Beard who developed that economic interpretation of the Civil War which deeply influenced the thinking of thousands of young Americans of the last two decades. According to the Beards' theory, the Civil War was at bottom a struggle of two organized and self-conscious economic groups — the northern industrial and business interests and the southern planter aristocracy — for the possession of the government of the United States. These two groups, each dominating its own section, had economic and political aims that were so completely antithetical as to make war between them inevitable. To the Beards, as our excerpt from their work makes clear, all other issues, such as states' rights or slavery, were "linguistic devices" shaped by the basic economic conflict. On the other hand, the danger of oversimplification in an economic interpretation of the Civil War is pointed out in the selection from Philip S. Foner's *Business and Slavery.*

Still another school of interpretation has been influenced by the great interest of historians in the development of nationalism in the last two centuries. Many American historians, including Edward Channing, Jesse Carpenter, Harry J. Carman, Samuel E. Morison, and Henry S. Commager, have dealt in one way or another with the development of a separate southern nationalism, and its nature has recently been restudied in its relation to nineteenth century European romantic nationalism by Rollin G. Osterweis, who concludes that it was a key element in bringing about the Civil War. A chapter from his *Romanticism and Nationalism in the Old South* is our final selection.

Many Americans will be tempted to resolve the conflict of opinions about the causes of the Civil War with an eclectic interpretation which combines such factors as southern nationalism, sectional economic rivalry, political and constitutional theories, overbold and/or unskillful leadership, and slavery. They may even propose deliberately that a combination of these elements with the right timing and intensity produced an explosion just as do the components of an atomic bomb when brought into critical proximity. Others will regard such eclecticism as an evasion of the issue and will maintain that in the mass of discernible issues there is some unconditional factor such as slavery which shaped and moved all other issues.

At any rate, the question of the causes of the Civil War is only a particular case in the perplexing problem of human conflict. Men have wrestled in every age with the question of whether there are and always will be fundamental and irreconcilable differences in life, or whether through analysis and education man may learn to control conflicts so as to avoid the material waste and human suffering of war. We, in our own time, face a situation in the world which is not too different from that which Americans faced in the 1850's.

[NOTE: The statement by Harold U. Faulkner on p. x is quoted from *American Political and Social History* (5th ed., New York, 1948), p. 353, by permission of Appleton-Century-Crofts, Inc.]

CONTENTS

The Clash of Issues

A long-accepted view:

"Of the American Civil War it may safely be asserted that there was a single cause, slavery."

— James F. Rhodes

A modern restatement of this older view:

"Slavery was at the very heart of our disequilibrium. It was the core of the social, the economic, the political, and the constitutional conflicts."

— Bernard DeVoto

The author of a widely used textbook in American history demurs:

"Slavery was the surface issue; the real conflict went deeper. . . . The economic forces let loose by the Industrial Revolution were finding full play and were beating irresistibly upon a one-sided and rather static civilization in the South."

— Harold U. Faulkner

A student of cultural nationalism states his theory:

"By 1860, the boundaries of the United States encompassed two nations. A people whose way of life had received direction from the plantation system and the institution of slavery began to manifest a group consciousness suggestive of nineteenth century European Romantic Nationalism. Once this group consciousness had taken hold, a war for Southern independence became more than a possibility."

— Rollin G. Osterweis

Another dissenting view:

"If one word or phrase were selected to account for the war, that word would not be slavery, or economic grievance, or state rights, or diverse civilizations. It would have to be such a word as fanaticism."

— J. G. Randall

James F. Rhodes: ANTECEDENTS OF THE AMERICAN CIVIL WAR, 1850–1860

GARDINER'S title "History of Our Great Civil War" has always struck me as apt. A historian so careful in his use of adjectives could not have adopted one so expressive without reflection. The English Civil War was great in itself and its consequences, and, though it may not convey as important lessons to the whole civilized world as did that one of which Thucydides was the historian, yet for its influence on American colonial life and on the development of our history to the formation of our Constitution, it is for us a more pregnant study. Moreover Gardiner's history of it is a model for the historian of our Civil War.

There is risk in referring any historic event to a single cause. Lecky entitled his celebrated chapter, "Causes of the French Revolution." Social and political, as well as religious, reasons, according to Gardiner, brought on the Great Civil War. Thucydides, on the other hand, though he did indeed set forth the "grounds of quarrel," stated his own belief that "the real though unavowed cause" of the war was "the growth of the Athenian power." And of the American Civil War it may safely be asserted that there was a single cause, slavery. In 1862 John Stuart Mill in *Fraser's Magazine*, and Professor Cairnes in a pamphlet on the Slave Power, presented this view to the English public with force, but it is always difficult to get to the bottom of a foreign dispute, and it is not surprising that many failed to comprehend the real nature of the conflict. When in July, 1862, William E. Forster said in the House of Commons that he believed it was generally acknowledged that slavery was the cause of the war, he was answered with cries, "No, no!" and "The tariff!" Because the South was for free trade and the North for a protective tariff this was a natural retort, though proceeding from a misconception, as a reference to the most acute tariff crisis in our history will show.

In 1832, South Carolina, by act of her Convention legally called, declared that the tariff acts passed by Congress in 1828 and 1832 were "null, void, no law," and that no duties enjoined by those acts should be paid or permitted to be paid in the State of South Carolina. It is a significant fact that she failed to induce any of her sister Southern States to act with her. By the firmness of President Jackson and a conciliatory disposition on the part of the high tariff party the act of nullification was never put in force; but the whole course of the incident and the yielding of South Carolina demonstrated that the American Union could not be broken up by a tariff dispute. Natural causes since 1832 have modified the geographical character of the controversy. The production of sugar in Louisiana, the mining of coal and the manufacture of iron in a number of Southern States have caused their senators and representatives to listen kindly to pleas for a protective tariff.

Here is a further illustration of the unique character of the divisional or, as we should say, sectional dispute concerning slavery. Sixteen years ago, the money question, the demand for the free coinage of silver, took on a sectional character in arraying the West and the South against the East, but the advocates of the gold standard always had a hearing and a party in the States devoted to silver. But after 1850, there was no antislavery party in the South and men advocating even the gradual abolition of slavery would not have been suffered to speak. Again, in 1896, natural causes had play; they took from the dispute about the money standard its sectional character. The disappearance of the grasshoppers that ate the wheat and maize, the breaking of the severe drought of the preceding years, the extension further west of the rain belt, good crops of cotton, maize and wheat with a good demand, brought prosperity to the farmers and with it a belief that the gold standard best served their interests.

Some of our younger writers, impressed with the principle of nationality that prevailed in Europe during the last half of the nineteenth century, have read into our conflict European conditions and asserted that the South stood for disunion in her doctrine of States' rights and that the war came because the North took up the gage of battle to make of the United States a nation. I shall have occasion to show the potency of the Union sentiment as an aid to the destruction of slavery, but when events are reduced to their last elements, it plainly appears that the doctrine of States' rights and secession was invoked by the South to save slavery, and by a natural antagonism, the North upheld the Union because the fight for its preservation was the first step toward the abolition of negro servitude. The question may be isolated by the incontrovertible statement that if the negro had never been brought to America, our Civil War could not have occurred.

The problem was a tougher one than had confronted Rome even if we regard as justified Mommsen's dire arraignment of slavery in his brilliant chapter. "Riches and misery," he wrote, "in close league drove the Italians out of Italy and filled the Peninsula partly with swarms of slaves, partly with awful silence." In the South, the slaves belonged to an inferior race; the gulf is deep between the white race and the black. I wish, said James Madison, that I might work a miracle. I would make all the blacks white. I could then in a day abolish slavery. Just before the war, a lunatic in an asylum near Boston, who took great interest in the different proposed compromises and solutions of the insoluble controversy, finally announced, I have found it! I know what will prevent the war. Countless pails of whitewash, innumerable brushes; make the negroes white!

I purpose devoting my first lecture to the antecedents of our Civil War and I shall begin the account with a statement of conditions in 1850. The issue of the war with Mexico gave the United States a large amount of new territory, known then as California and New Mexico, which under the Mexican law were free from slavery and ought to remain so unless this condition were removed by express enactment. But Calhoun, Senator from South Carolina, with ascendant influence over the Southern mind, had a theory to fit the occasion. He said that when the sovereignty of Mexico was succeeded by that of the United States, the American Constitution applied to the new territory, and as it recognized slavery, so it permitted slave owners to take their slaves into California and New Mexico; in other words it legalized slavery. This new doctrine was eagerly embraced by the South. But the North, believing that slavery was wrong, demanded that the general government prohibit it in the new territory, and although the letter of the Constitution was silent on this subject, legislative precedent amply supported this demand as strictly constitutional. California for herself resolved the question. The discovery of gold promoted the settlement of this territory by a mass of seekers of fortune, many of them outcasts and vagrants, while others, though rough, hardy men, loving cards and drink, had a native sense of justice which demanded fair play. The speedy settlement of this hitherto unknown country led De Quincey to say, "She is going ahead at a rate that beats Sindbad and Gulliver"; and Bret Harte has feelingly portrayed the early settlers and their surroundings in "Tales of the Argonauts," "Luck of Roaring Camp" and "Outcasts of Poker Flat." The quasi-military government and the survival of the Mexican municipal authority did not prevent California from reaching the verge of anarchy and a majority were earnest that Congress should institute a stable territorial government, which it still failed to do because of the difference about slavery. Eventually the better class of immigrants, who were constantly increasing, took the lead in forming a State government. A Convention regularly chosen adopted a Constitution modelled after the constitutions of New York and Iowa and no objection whatever was made to the clause in the bill of rights which forever prohibited slavery in the State. This was done from no moral motive, as men from the South, believing that slavery was right, joined with Northerners, who believed it wrong, in this prohibition, because they thought it would be out of place in the new country. As an old mountaineer argued in a harangue to the crowd, "In a country where every white man made a slave of himself there was no use in keeping niggers." Armed with her excellent Constitution, California then proceeded in a regular manner to make a natural and just demand. In the parlance of the day, she knocked at the doors of Congress for admission into the Union, but failed to receive a general welcome for the sole reason that she had prohibited slavery.

As slavery was out of tune with the nineteenth century, the States that held fast to it played a losing game. This was evident from the greater increase of population at the North. When Washington became President (1789), the population of the two sections was nearly equal, but thirty-one years later, in a total of less than ten millions there was a difference of 667,000 in favor of the North, and when, twelve years later still, the immigration from Europe began, the preponderance of the North continued to increase. The South repelled immigrants for the reason that freemen would not work with slaves. In the House of Representatives, chosen on the basis of numerical population, the North, at each decennial census and apportionment, gained largely on the South, whose stronghold was the Senate. Each State, irrespective of population, had two senators, and since the formation of the Constitution, States had been admitted in pairs by a tacit agreement, each free State being counterbalanced by a slave State. The admission of California which would disturb this equilibrium was resisted by the South with a spirit of determination made bitter by disappointment over California's spontaneous act. The Mexican War had been for the most part a Southern war; the South, as Lowell made Hosea Biglow say, was "after bigger pens to cram with slaves," and now she saw this magnificent domain of California escaping her clutches. She had other grievances which, from the point of view of a man of 1850 reverencing the letter of the Constitution, were undoubtedly well founded, but the whole dispute really hinged on the belief of the South that slavery was right and the belief of the majority of Northerners that it was wrong.

At the time of the formation of the Constitution the two sections were not greatly at variance. A large number of Southern men, among them their ablest and best leaders, thought slavery was a moral and political evil to be got rid of gradually. In due time, the foreign slave trade was prohibited, but the Yankee invention of the cotton-gin made slavery apparently profitable in the culture of cotton on the virgin soil of the new States in the South; and Southern opinion changed. From being regarded as an evil, slavery began to be looked upon as the only possible condition of the existence of the two races side by side and by 1850 the feeling had grown to be that slavery was "no evil, no scourge, but a great religious, social and moral blessing." As modern society required hewers of wood and drawers of water, the slave system of the South, so the argument ran, was superior to the industrial system of England, France and the North.

In 1831, William Lloyd Garrison began his crusade against slavery. In a weekly journal, the *Liberator*, published in Boston, he preached with fearless emphasis that slavery was wrong and, though his immediate followers were never many, he set people to thinking about the question, so that six years later Daniel Webster, one of our greatest statesmen with a remarkable power of expression, said, the subject of slavery "has not only attracted attention as a question of politics, but it has struck a far deeper-toned chord. It has arrested the religious feeling of the country; it has taken strong hold on the consciences of men." In the nineteen years before 1850 the opinion constantly gained ground at the North that slavery was an evil and that its existence at the South was a blot on the national honor.

In 1850, there were at the South 347,000 slaveholders out of a white population of six millions, but the head and centre of the oligarchy was to be found amongst the large planters, possessors of fifty or more slaves, whose elegance, luxury and hospitality are recited in tales of travellers, over whose estates and lives the light of romance and poetry has been profusely shed; of these, there were less than eight thousand. Around them clustered the fashionable circles of the cities, composed of merchants, doctors and lawyers, a society seen to the best advantage in New Orleans, Charleston and Richmond. The men composing this oligarchy were high-spirited gentlemen, with a keen sense of honor showing itself in hatred of political corruption, resentment of personal attack by speech or by pen, to the length of the fatal duel, and a reverence for and readiness to protect female virtue. Most of them were well educated and had a taste for reading; but they avoided American literature as emanating mostly from New England, the hotbed of abolitionism, and preferred the earlier English literature to that of the nineteenth century. But their ability manifested itself not at all in letters or in art, but ran entirely to law and politics, in which they were really eminent. English travellers before the Civil War liked the Southerners for their aristocratic bearing and enjoyed their conversation, which was not redolent of trade and the dollar, like much that they heard at the North. It is obvious that men of this stamp could not be otherwise than irritated when Northern speeches, books and newspapers were full of the charge that they were living in the daily practice of evil, that negro chattel slavery was cruel, unjust and barbaric. This irritation expressed itself in recrimination and insolent demands at the same time that it helped to bring them to the belief that property in negroes was as right and sacred as the ownership of horses and mules.

In 1850, the South repeatedly asserted that she must have her rights or she would secede from the Union; and her action eleven years later proved that this was not an idle threat. She would submit to the admission of California provided she received certain guarantees. There resulted the Compromise of 1850, proposed by Henry Clay and supported by Daniel Webster and finally enacted by Congress. Under it California came in free. Slavery was not prohibited in New Mexico. Webster argued that such prohibition was unnecessary as the territory was not adapted to slavery. "I would not," he said, "take pains uselessly to reaffirm an ordinance of nature, nor to reenact the will of God." The South obtained a more stringent Fugitive Slave Law. Most of the negroes yearned for freedom, and, while their notions of geography were vague, they knew that freedom lay in the direction of the north star, and with that guidance a thousand escaped yearly into the free States. The rendition of fugitive slaves was a right under the Constitution, and as the South maintained that the law of 1793 was inadequate, she demanded one more stringent. In the end, a bill based on the draft of James Mason (the Mason of Mason-Slidell fame) was enacted. It ran counter to the Roman maxim that, if a question arose about the civil status of a person, he was presumed to be free until proved to be a slave, thus laying the burden of proof on the master and giving the benefit of the doubt to the weaker party. Under this Act of ours the negro had no chance: the meshes of the law were artfully contrived to aid the master and entrap the alleged slave. By an extraordinary provision, the commissioner who determined the matter received a fee of ten dollars if he adjudged the negro to slavery and one half of that amount if he held the fugitive to be a free man. The real purpose of the law was not so much to recover the runaway negroes as it was to irritate the North (or, in the current figure of speech, to crack the whip over the heads of Northern men) by its rigorous enforcement. To this end being admirably designed, it became one of the minor influences that brought the North to her final resolute stand against the extension of slavery.

Mason was the sort of man to think that he had done a clever thing when, in drawing an act to enforce the constitutional right of the South, he made its enforcement needlessly irritating to the North. But it proved a menace and a plague to the section it was intended to benefit. For the Fugitive Slave Law inspired Harriet Beecher Stowe to write Uncle Tom's Cabin, the greatest of American novels which, in the interest that it aroused and the influence that it exerted, has not unfitly been compared to La nouvelle Héloïse. Though the author possessed none of Rousseau's force and grace of style, her novel, and the play founded on it, could not have secured the attention of England and France unless its human element had been powerfully presented. Macaulay wrote that "on the whole, it is the most valuable addition that America has made to English literature." England and her colonies bought a million and a half copies. Two London theatres produced the play. Three daily newspapers in Paris published it as a serial and the Parisians filled two theatres nightly to laugh at Topsy and weep at the hard fate of Uncle Tom. Many other stories were written to exhibit the wrongs of the negro under chattel slavery, but they are all forgotten. Slavery, in the destruction of which Uncle Tom's Cabin had a potent influence, is gone, but the novel, published in 1852, is still read and the drama acted, telling the present generation of the great political and social revolution wrought in their father's time.

From 1852 to 1860, the year in which Lincoln was elected President, the influence of this story on Northern thought was immense. The author had made no effort to suppress the good side of slavery, but had shown an intelligent sympathy for the well-meaning masters, who had been reared under the system; at the same time she had laid bare the injustice, cruelty and horror of the white man's ownership of the negro with a fidelity to nature that affected every reader. The election of Lincoln is a great fact in the destruction of slavery and, in gaining voters for him, Uncle Tom's Cabin was one of the effective influences. It made a strong appeal to women, and the mothers' opinion was a potent educator during these eight years; boys who had read Uncle Tom's Cabin in their early teens reached the voting age at a time when they could give slavery a hard knock.

The Compromise of 1850 was an adroit device, as compromises go, and with the exception of the indefensible portions of the Fugitive Slave Law, was fair to both sections. It abated the antislavery agitation at the North and the threats of disunion at the South and would probably have maintained quiet between the two sections for a considerable period had not an able Democratic senator opened the question afresh in 1854.

Slavery, as a sectional issue, had first claimed the attention of Congress in 1820 in the form of a proposition to admit Missouri as a slave State. "This momentous question," wrote Jefferson from his retirement, "like a fire-bell in the night awakened and filled me with terror. I considered it at once as the knell of the Union." The result of the agitation was the Missouri Compromise. Missouri was admitted as a slave State, but her Southern boundary of 36°30′ was henceforward taken as the line between slavery and freedom in the rest of the great territory of the Louisiana Purchase. North of that line slavery was forever prohibited.

In 1854, Stephen A. Douglas, a senator from Illinois, filled the public eye. Though he had never received any systematic education, he was a man of natural parts and had achieved a considerable success at the bar; then, finding politics more to his liking than the law, he had been able so to commend himself to his community that his political advancement was rapid and, up to a point, practically continuous. He had become one of the leaders of the Democratic party and craved the presidency; being no believer in the maxim that everything comes to him who waits, he naturally adopted the boldest methods for gratifying his restless ambition. As chairman of the Committee on Territories and leader of the Democrats in the Senate, he introduced a bill for the organization of the territories of Nebraska and Kansas, one clause in which provided for the repeal of the Missouri Compromise of 1820. Here was an open bid for Southern support in his contest for the presidency. His bill became a law and the slavery question was opened anew. For instead of being closed to slavery by formal Congressional act, these territories were now open to settlers from both North and South, the one bringing their horses and mules, and the others having the privilege of bringing their slaves as well.

The North was indignant at this violation of a solemn compact by a movement initiated by one of her own sons. As I look back upon this episode, with every disposition to be fair to Douglas and not unmindful of apologies for his conduct that conscientious historical students have made, I believe that he merits strong condemnation from history. By his act was revived a perilous dispute that was thought to have been settled. Douglas loved his country and reverenced the Constitution, but he could not see the evil of slavery; he did not appreciate that it was out of tune with his century. Not intending, at first, to go the full length of repealing the Missouri Compromise, he found that, upon opening the question, he had invoked a sentiment at the South that demanded full measure. To retreat would be cowardly, even ridiculous. He must go forward or give up his position as a leader. Therefore he demanded, in the end without evasion, the repeal of the Missouri Compromise and supported his measure by adroit but specious reasoning. He stood for the doctrine which went by the high-sounding name of popular sovereignty and meant that the people of the territories themselves should determine whether slavery should be protected or prohibited within their borders, and he accordingly carried the notion of local government to an unworkable and dangerous extreme, considering that the question involved was slavery. Give the people a chance to decide, he argued continually. "If they wish slavery, they have a right to it." "I care not whether slavery is voted down or voted up."

Of parliamentarians, in the English sense of the word, Douglas is one of the cleverest in our annals. The conduct of his measure through the Senate, where he was opposed by men of remarkable ability and where the closure does not obtain, was a master stroke of parliamentary management. With the help of the President and the zeal of Southern representatives, who were quick to see their advantage, the House adopted Douglas's measure despite the rise of indignant sentiment in the North at the betrayal of a sacred pledge. This outburst of public opinion was predicted on the day that the Senate passed the bill. On that sombre March morning of 1854, when the cannon from the navy-yard was booming out the legislative victory, Senator Chase, an earnest opponent of the bill, said to his intimate and sympathizing friend, Senator Sumner, as they walked away from the Capitol together, "They celebrate a present victory but the echoes they awake will never rest until slavery itself shall die."

Chase was right. The antislavery men, a powerful majority of the North, deemed the bill an outrage. From the press and the public platform, from the "stump," as we say, in grove or park, came emphatic condemnation of the conduct of Douglas and of the act of Congress. Douglas's unpopularity in the North was intense and widespread. It was then a common practice to burn in effigy the public man whose course was disapproved. "I could travel," said Douglas, "from Boston to Chicago by the light of my own effigies." Arriving in Chicago, his home, he gave notice that he would address his constituents, but his opponents went to the meeting and, by cries of execration, denied him a hearing.

Like Mason's Fugitive Slave Bill Douglas's repeal of the Missouri Compromise reacted to the detriment of its author. It destroyed his chance for the presidency. It brought about the formation of the Republican party. On the 1st of January, 1854, the two chief parties in the country were the Democratic and Whig, the Democratic having the presidency and a good majority in both the Senate and the House. There was a third party, the Free-Soil, which, holding as its cardinal doctrine opposition to slavery, sometimes held the balance of power in closely contested Northern States, but which had only a small representation in Congress. The repeal of the Missouri Compromise roused the dormant antislavery feeling in the country and brought home to many the conviction that a new party should be formed to unite Whigs, antislavery Democrats and Free-Soilers in their resistance to the aggression of the slave power. Seward's ability and political experience seemed to mark him out for leadership, but he was a devoted Whig and, as the Northern Whigs had, to a man, opposed the repeal of the Missouri Compromise and would form the predominant element in the new partnership, he thought that all antislavery men should enlist under their banner. Westerners thought differently and, being less trammelled by political organizations than their Eastern cousins, proceeded to inaugurate the movement that was really demanded by the posture of affairs. Five weeks after the repeal of the Missouri Compromise, a large body of earnest, intelligent and reputable men, the leading citizens of the State of Michigan, came together at Jackson and, as the largest hall was inadequate for their accommodation, they met in a grove of famous oaks in the outskirts of the village. Here they resolved to suspend all differences regarding economic or administrative policy, to act cordially and faithfully in unison with all opposed to the extension of slavery and to be known as Republicans until the end of the contest. Other States followed this example.

The year 1854 was one of political and moral excitement. Though undoubtedly the original impulse came from the repeal of the Missouri Compromise, all the ensuing agitation did not turn on the question of slavery. The temperance question entered into politics; more conspicuous than this was the so-called Know-nothing movement, the object of which was a political proscription of foreigners, especially Roman Catholics. Important as were their acts for a twelvemonth or so, the Know-nothings need not divert us from the main issue which, as we study it in the elections of members for the House of Representatives in the autumn of 1854, was the repeal of the Missouri Compromise — Should it be upheld or denounced? In this contest the Northern press had a marked influence and, in its warm advocacy of the cause of freedom, wrote for itself a noble chapter. The foremost journalist of the day was Horace Greeley, who exerted his peculiar influence through the *New York Weekly Tribune,* which was estimated to have half a million readers, many of whom looked upon it as a kind of political bible. The revolution in public sentiment was strikingly disclosed in the elections of

1854. In the House, which had repealed the Missouri Compromise, the Democrats had been in a majority of 84; in the succeeding one, they were in a minority of 75. Of forty-two Northern Democrats who had voted for the Repeal only seven were reelected. While the North deemed the Repeal an outrage, the South hailed it with joy. Believing that slavery was right and that negroes were property, she thought that an equal privilege in the territory now in question was her due. Douglas in his bill separated the vast territory into two parts, the northern part Nebraska, the southern Kansas. The South regarded this provision as indicating an intention to give her a new slave State in Kansas while Nebraska was entitled to freedom. But under the Douglas scheme of popular sovereignty the people of the territory should themselves decide whether or not they would have slavery. The actual result was a contest between the South and the North on the plains of Kansas. The adjoining slave State, Missouri, sent thither a number of settlers who, for the most part, wished merely to better their condition; and, at the same time, in response to the pioneering spirit of the age, a large emigration from the Western free States took place. Behind these natural movements were an organized effort in Missouri to make Kansas a slave State and an Emigrant Aid Company in New England, whose purpose was to make her free. At the first election for a territorial legislature, a mob of five thousand Missourians, armed to the teeth, marched into Kansas, took possession of the ballot-boxes and chose the proslavery candidates, who, on their meeting, legalized slavery, and, to maintain it, adopted a code of laws of exceptional harshness and severity. Meanwhile New England emigrants reenforced the original Northern settlers until there was a respectable free-state party wisely led. These repudiated the territorial legislature as illegal, organized at once a state government and applied to Congress for admission into the Union, so that there existed in Kansas at the same time two governments and two sets of people directly hostile to each other. The President and the Senate supported the proslavery party, while the majority of the House, elected during the indignant protest against Douglas's Repeal of the Missouri Compromise, were on the side of the free-state settlers.

The cause of Kansas was declared to be the cause of the South and appeals were made for emigrants and for slaves. One of the Missouri leaders said, "If we can get two thousand slaves actually lodged in Kansas, our success is certain." But all the negroes were wanted in the cotton States for the production of cotton. Moreover, there was a lack of means in the South properly to equip and arm the young hardy men who were desired for the conflict. The most significant result of the appeals by the press and political leaders was the arming and equipment of two hundred eighty men raised in three of the cotton States, known from its leader as Buford's battalion, who after a blessing from the Methodist pastor and a promise of Bibles from the Baptist, left Montgomery for Kansas to fight for the cause of slavery. At about the same time a meeting was held in a New Haven church to collect money for a company of seventy-nine emigrants who should go to Kansas to battle for freedom. A number of ministers and several of the Yale College faculty were present. Fifty Sharpe's rifles were wanted. Professor Silliman subscribed for one, the pastor of the church for a second, and, as the subscription went on, Henry Ward Beecher, a celebrated pulpit orator, said that if twenty-five were promised, his Plymouth Church would give the rest. Henceforward the favorite arms of the Northern emigrants, Sharpe's rifles, were known as "Beecher's Bibles." The men who bore them were called in the cotton States "Hireling emigrants, poured in to extinguish this new hope of the South"; at the North the Missouri invaders were called "border ruffians," whilst their allies, Buford's battalion, were scarcely in better odor. When feelings ran so high in the peaceful portions of the country, it is little wonder that Kansas itself was soon in a state of civil war. At first the so-called "border ruffians" were the offenders, but when a free-state company under the leadership of John Brown had in one night on the Pottawatomie deliberately and cruelly murdered five proslavery men, it could no longer be said that the work of violence was all on one side. Guerilla bands of both parties wandered over the territory and engaged one another at sight. No frugal settler of either party was safe from pillage at the hands of marauders from the other camp. Women and children fled the territory. Men slept on their arms. Highway robbery and rapine prevailed over all the country-side; "the smoke of burning dwellings darkened the atmosphere." As the proslavery faction had the Federal government on its side, it claimed to be the party of law and order and in that name were committed its depredations, whilst the other faction killed and robbed in the name of liberty. Yet, in a balancing of acts and character, the free-state adherents of 1856 are superior to the proslavery partisans in everything that goes to make up industrious and law-abiding citizens. The free-state men lost the larger amount of property and the destruction caused by the proslavery faction was much the greater.

Kansas was engrossing the attention of Congress when there took place in the Senate an incident that profoundly affected Northern sentiment. Charles Sumner, Senator from Massachusetts, had spoken on "The Crime against Kansas," making use of much exaggeration and turgid rhetoric in his invective against the operations of the slave power. It was not this portion of his speech, however, that was responsible for its unfortunate sequel, but a bitter personal attack, with insulting allusions, on Butler, a Southern aristocrat and Senator from South Carolina. Two days later, after the adjournment of the Senate, while Sumner was sitting at his desk writing letters, he was approached by Preston Brooks, a representative from South Carolina, who declared that he had libelled South Carolina and his relative, Senator Butler. When he had spoken, Brooks raised his cane and struck Sumner on the head with all his might, continuing to strike until he had stunned and blinded his victim. The cane broke; even then he rained blows with the butt on the defenceless head. Sumner instinctively wrenched the desk from its fastenings, stood up, and with wildly directed efforts attempted to defend himself. Brooks struck him again and again. At last Sumner, reeling, staggering backwards and sideways, fell to the floor, bleeding profusely and covered with his blood.

Sumner had an iron constitution and excellent health, but his spinal column was affected so that he must spend the next three and a half years in search of a cure. He received medical treatment in Washington, Boston, London and Paris, but never regained his former physical vigor. By an almost unanimous vote of the Massachusetts Legislature he was reelected to the Senate where his empty seat was eloquent for his cause.

Not until December, 1859, was he able to resume and steadily pursue his senatorial career.

The assault struck the North with horror and indignation, while in the slave States it was approved by the press and by the people. The assailant was spoken of as the courageous and noble Brooks; indeed the South rallied to him as the champion of their cause.

As the Senate was democratic and the House republican, Congress failed to agree on a bill that would dispose of the Kansas trouble. The contest in the legislative chambers was then transferred to the country and the opportunity for a verdict from the people was at hand, inasmuch as a President and a House of Representatives was to be chosen in this year of 1856. The Democrats nominated Buchanan in preference to Douglas, because Buchanan had been out of the country as minister to England during these years and was not associated with the repeal of the Missouri Compromise and the consequent disturbance in Kansas. The Republican National Convention was an exceptionally earnest and patriotic body of men, yet it made an unfortunate nomination for President in Colonel Fremont, who lacked both the ability and the character demanded of the leader of so righteous a cause. But the Convention registered the popular will. It was a boon that he failed of election, as he was unfit to cope with the secession of the Southern States, which would certainly have ensued. The Republican declaration of principles was an improvement on the candidate. It demanded the admission of Kansas as a free State and declared it to be both the right and duty of Congress to prohibit slavery in the territories. The Republicans made an enthusiastic canvass, condemning the repeal of the Missouri Compromise and pointing to "bleeding Kansas" as its result. But Buchanan was elected President, and the Democrats regained control of the House of Representatives. As they still had the Senate by a majority of 12, they were in full possession of the executive and legislative branches of the government.

Our government is singular in its complete separation of the executive, legislative and judicial powers. Under any polity, as Mr. Bryce observed, we must come to the people at last; yet each branch of our government emanates from the people in a different manner. Districts of a population of 93,000 (I am speaking of 1856; our congressional districts are now much larger) elect the members of the House of Representatives. The voters of each State choose a legislature which elects two senators.[1] The President is chosen through a method of indirect election, by the people of the United States, and he appoints the justices of the Supreme Court, who, however, must be confirmed by the Senate and who have a life tenure.

For three years the national legislature and executive had endeavored to solve the slavery problem with conspicuous failure. Now the Supreme Court was to try its hand. Its Chief Justice has great power in directing the consideration of the Court to constitutional questions which may arise in any case before it. The present Chief, Taney, had been on the Bench for twenty-two years and had gained a solid reputation for accurate knowledge of law and clearness of statement. Being of broadly patriotic temper, he made up his mind that his Court could settle the slavery question, and, in a case where it was necessary only to determine

[1] [The present direct election of Senators was instituted by the Seventeenth Amendment in 1913. – Ed.]

whether a certain negro named Dred Scott was slave or freeman, he delivered a carefully prepared opinion in which he asserted that "the right of property in a slave is distinctly and expressly affirmed in the Constitution"; that Congress had no more power over slave property than over property of any other kind; consequently the Missouri Compromise Act "is not warranted by the Constitution and is therefore void." Five judges agreed with Taney and these made two-thirds of the Court. This decision which neutralized the Republican doctrine that Congress had the power to prohibit slavery in the territories, was a blow to those Republican leaders who were good lawyers and who reverenced the Supreme Court. It was met in the commonsense way by Abraham Lincoln, who declared that the Republicans offered no resistance to the decision, but, believing it to be erroneous, would do their best to get the Court to overrule it as it had previously overruled other decisions.

This so-called Dred Scott opinion was delivered two days after the inauguration of Buchanan, and though it did not dispose of the Kansas question, it gave a theoretical basis to slavery in the territories and furnished a strong support for the next move of the slave power.

The effort to make Kansas an actual slave territory had failed, as it had now within its borders only 200 or 300 slaves; but, as there were sixteen free to fifteen slave States, the proslavery party eagerly desired the political power of another State – its two senators and one or more representatives – to restore the equilibrium existing before 1850. A plan to this end was promptly devised. Originating probably with Southerners of high position in Washington, it found ready instruments in Kansas. A sham election resulted in a constitutional convention, which framed a Constitution establishing slavery in the most unequivocal terms and which, as it could not avoid the time-honored precedent of submitting the Constitution to a popular vote, provided for a submission of it that, in the words of the Democratic governor of the territory, was "a vile fraud, a base counterfeit and a wretched device" to prevent the people from deciding whether or not they would have slavery. For the Convention did not dare to provide for a fair election, as the proslavery advocates would have been outvoted three to one. President Buchanan, though from a Northern State, had a great admiration for Southern politicians whose persuasion and threats induced him to support this plan, which was known as the Lecompton scheme.

The proceeding was a travesty of the doctrine of popular sovereignty, and when the Senate met in December, 1857, Douglas boldly denounced it. His manner was haughty and defiant as he set himself in opposition to his party, the Democratic, which was strongly entrenched in all three branches of the government, and he did not hesitate to characterize the scheme "as a trick, a fraud upon the rights of the people." Despite Douglas's opposition, the Democratic Senate voted to admit Kansas as a State under her proslavery constitution, but to this the House, in closer contact with the people, would not agree. The excitement in Washington was intense, and, during a heated all-night session of the House, an altercation between a Southern and Northern representative resulted in a fisticuff, in which thirty men were engaged, but no weapons drawn. In the end a compromise was agreed upon between the Senate and the House, the effect of which was to offer to Kansas a large amount of public lands if she would accept the Lecompton constitution. By a vote of 11,300 to 1800 she rejected the bribe and thus determined that slavery should not exist in Kansas. But the affair left an irreconcilable breach in the Democratic party.

We are now in the year 1858, in the spring of which year Douglas was the best-known and most popular man in the North, so effectively had he won back public esteem by his resistance to the Lecompton project. The relations between him and the Republicans in Congress were cordial and the possibility that their party should nominate him as their candidate for the presidency two years hence was considered by no means out of the question. Seward was coquetting with him but had no idea of stepping aside in his favor if the conditions were propitious for Republican success. Douglas must stand this year for reelection as senator from Illinois and the leading Eastern Republicans, nearly every Republican senator and many representatives desired that their party should make no opposition to him. Greeley in his powerful journal warmly favored his return to the Senate; but the Republicans in Illinois, under the lead of Abraham Lincoln, protested against it.

The son of a shiftless poor white of the slave State of Kentucky, Lincoln was brought up in that State and the southern part of Indiana, moving to Illinois when he was twenty-one. The southern Indiana of that day might have suggested the Eden of Martin Chuzzlewit. Its farms and villages were rude and ill-kept; fever and ague were unrepressed; the most ordinary refinements of human existence were lacking even to what would be considered there to-day the actual necessaries of civilization. Lincoln said that the story of his early life was told in a single sentence of Gray's Elegy, —

"The short and simple annals of the poor."

His schooling was necessarily meagre, but he had an active mind and an extraordinary power of application. He was a thorough student of the Bible and Shakespeare and mastered the first six books of Euclid. Reading few books, he thought long and carefully on what he read, and his opinions on all subjects were generally the result of severe study and profound reflection. He studied law and at the age of twenty-eight began practice; but his interest in politics was so deep as to brook no enduring rival. He loved and believed in the common people; he amused them and interested them in himself. His early associates were American born, dwellers in village and lonely farm and the stories he told them were of the order that there prevails; if they were amusing, he cared little if they were coarse as well. A frequenter of the tavern, he used neither spirits nor tobacco; his personal morals were good. He served one term in the Illinois legislature, another in the United States House of Representatives, but not belonging to the dominant party in his State, he failed to remain continuously in the public service. He reached a high rank in his profession, being esteemed the strongest jury lawyer in Illinois; but he was a bad advocate in an unjust cause. The repeal of the Missouri Compromise diverted his attention from law to politics, and a speech, in which he demolished Douglas's political and historical sophistry, made him the leader of the Republicans in his State. Lincoln was then nearly elected United States senator, but although deeply disappointed, he, with rare magnanimity and judgment, withdrew in favor of another candidate, to prevent the defeat of the cause. Intensely ambitious, he nevertheless loved truth and justice better than political place and power. At twenty-four he had been dubbed "honest Abe." At no time in his eventful life did he do anything to cast a shadow of discredit on this epithet sprung from the rude soil of Illinois.

At the age of forty-nine, Lincoln was hardly known beyond the confines of his own State or, wherever known in the East, was regarded as a "backwoods lawyer"; yet he stood forth to contest the senatorship with the most formidable debater in the country. He gave the keynote of the campaign in the most carefully prepared speech that he had ever made, addressed to the Republican State Convention, which had unanimously nominated him as the candidate of their party for senator. "'A house divided against itself cannot stand,'" he said. "I believe this government cannot endure permanently half slave and half free. . . . Either the opponents of slavery will arrest the further spread of it and place it where the public mind shall rest in the belief that it is in the course of ultimate extinction; or its advocates will push it forward till it shall become alike lawful in all the States, old as well as new, North as well as South."

When Douglas went to Chicago to open the campaign, his town gave him an enthusiastic reception, which contrasted strikingly with his home-coming four years earlier. In his first speech he attacked with great force Lincoln's "House-divided-against-itself" doctrine, which doctrine, though soon to be demonstrated in hard and cruel fact, had in 1858 not many adherents. When submitted to a dozen of Lincoln's political friends before public pronouncement, it had received the approval of only one, and after it was uttered, there was no doubt whatever that, inasmuch as it was in advance of his party's thought, it counted against him in his contest with Douglas. Douglas's progress through his State amounted to a continuous ovation. Travelling in special trains – an unusual proceeding at the time – the trains being drawn by decorated locomotives, he was met at each city by committees of escort, and, to the thunder of cannon and the music of brass bands, was driven under triumphal arches, on which was emblazoned the legend, "Popular Sovereignty." The blare and flare of the campaign were entirely to his liking, but they were merely the theatrical accessories of a truly remarkable actor.

His short and massive frame was surmounted by an enormous head, from which shone forth eyes of a penetrating keenness; his appearance alone justified the title of "little giant" long since given him. A melodious voice and a clear incisive enunciation combined with apt and forcible gestures to point the ingenious arguments that kindled a genuine enthusiasm in the sons of Illinois, whose admiration and love he had gained.

As a boy, I saw Douglas often at the house of my father, who was his warm personal and political friend. His great head seemed out of proportion to his short body, giving one the idea of a preponderance of the intellect. But he was not a reader and I do not remember ever seeing a book in his hand. Knowing little of Europe, he had absorbed the history of his own country and used this knowledge with ready skill. His winning manner was decisive with boys and he gained a hold on young voters, which he retained until Lincoln came to appeal to their moral sense.

Lincoln realized that the current was setting against him, but he felt no regret for his action in setting forth the positive doctrine of his opening speech. Believing that his adroit and plausible opponent could be better answered from a platform shared in common, he challenged him to a series of joint debates. He showed a profound confidence in his cause when he pitted himself against the man who in senatorial debate had got the better of Seward and Sumner and more recently had discomfited the champions of the Lecompton scheme. Lincoln was tall, gaunt, awkward; his face was dark, yellow, wrinkled and dry, voice shrill and unpleasant, movements shy and odd. In oratorical power and personal magnetism he was inferior to Douglas, but when he was warmed to his subject, his face glowed with the earnestness of conviction and he spoke with excellent result.

The joint debates, in different portions of the State, were seven; they are the most celebrated in our history. Illinois, though by no means fully aware of the crucial character of this contest, was nevertheless sufficiently aroused to turn out audiences of from five to twenty thousand at these day meetings, held in groves or on the prairie. Here Lincoln by his remorseless logic brought Douglas to bay. He showed that the slavery question was at rest when Douglas disturbed it by the Repeal of the Missouri Compromise. *Why could you not leave it alone?* he asked with emphasis. The doctrine of Popular Sovereignty was "*a living creeping lie.*" Douglas, he asserted, has undertaken to "build up a system of policy upon the basis of caring nothing about *the very thing that everybody does care the most about.*" The real issue, Lincoln truly declared, is whether slavery is right or wrong.

Each partisan who went to these meetings thought that his candidate got the better of the other. Douglas won the senatorship and for the moment the general opinion of the country that he had overpowered his antagonist in debate; but when the debates were published in book form, in 1860, opinion changed. Careful reading showed that in the dialectic contest Lincoln prevailed over Douglas; but he had an immense advantage in the just cause and the one to which public sentiment was tending.

The country now had four leaders, Lincoln, Douglas, Seward and Jefferson Davis. In October, 1858, Seward declared that there existed "an irrepressible conflict" between slavery and freedom. During the ensuing session of the Senate, Davis took the position that Congress was bound to protect slavery in the territories. This was a startling advance on the doctrine of Calhoun and the Supreme Court, who had simply maintained that Congress had no right or power to prohibit it. In truth the apparent necessity of fostering slavery had driven the Southerners to extreme ground. Having failed to secure Kansas or any other Western territory, they now made an effort to acquire Cuba, where the slave system already prevailed. Further acquisitions were hoped for in Mexico and Central America, where it was believed that slavery could be easily introduced. Moreover, as there were not negroes enough to cultivate the cotton, sugar and rice in the existing slave States, a large, possibly a predominant, party began to advocate the revival of the African slave trade. Indeed, during 1859, a large number of negroes were smuggled into the Southern States.

Towards the end of 1859, John Brown made his memorable attack on slavery. The method of the Republicans did not suit him; they respected slavery in the States where already established. The Abolitionists had "milk-and-water principles," issuing merely in talk. His own belief was that action was needed. Gathering eighteen followers, five of whom were negroes, he succeeded, on the cold, dark Sunday night of October 16, in capturing the United States armory, arsenal and rifle works at Harper's Ferry, Virginia, which were under civil, not military, guard. He expected the slaves of Virginia and the free negroes of the North to flock to his standard. These he would arm with pikes. Fortified against attack and subsisting on the enemy, he would make his name a terror throughout the South, so that property in man would become insecure and eventually slavery might thus be destroyed. When his friends urged the folly of attacking the State of Virginia, the United States government and the slave power with so small a band, he said, "If God be for us, who can be against us?" Imbued as he was with the lessons of the Old Testament, he undoubtedly imagined God would work for him the wonders that He had wrought for Joshua and Gideon.

The attempt, of course, failed quickly. During the Monday fighting was carried on with the people of Harper's Ferry; early next morning Colonel Robert E. Lee, at the head of a company of United States Marines, took Brown and four of his followers prisoners. Ten of them had been killed. Of the inhabitants and attacking parties five were killed and nine wounded.

Virginia was in an uproar. While the rabble would have liked to lynch Brown, men of education and position could not but admire his courage. He had a fair trial, was of course found guilty and, forty-five days later, hanged.

The Southerners believed that he had "whetted knives of butchery for their mothers, sisters, daughters and babes." To Northern statesmen, it was clear that he could have achieved success only by stirring up a servile war and unchaining passions such as had made the memory of San Domingo horrible. If this were the whole of his strange story, History could visit on Brown only the severest condemnation. But his words and behavior between arrest and execution, his composure on the scaffold under circumstances peculiarly distressing must give the ingenuous student pause. Though the contemporary raptures of Emerson and Victor Hugo now look preposterous, it must nevertheless be admitted that Brown suffered martyrdom for the anti-slavery cause. Nor is it possible to forget how Northern soldiers, as they marched to the front to fight for the freedom of the negro, were inspired by the stirring music and words, —

"John Brown's body lies a-mouldering
in the grave,
But his soul goes marching on."

Ulrich B. Phillips: THE CENTRAL THEME OF SOUTHERN HISTORY

AN Ohio River ferryman has a stock remark when approaching the right bank: "We are nearing the American shore." A thousand times has he said it with a gratifying repercussion from among his passengers; for its implications are a little startling. The northern shore is American without question; the southern is American with a difference. Kentucky had by slender pretense a star in the Confederate flag; for a time she was officially neutral; for all time her citizens have been self-consciously Kentuckians, a distinctive people. They are Southerners in main sentiment, and so are Marylanders and Missourians.

Southernism did not arise from any selectiveness of migration, for the sort of people who went to Virginia, Maryland, or Carolina were not as a group different from those who went to Pennsylvania or the West Indies. It does not lie in religion or language. It was not created by one-crop tillage, nor did agriculture in the large tend to produce a Southern scheme of life and thought. The Mohawk valley was for decades as rural as that of the Roanoke; wheat is as dominant in Dakota as cotton has ever been in Alabama; tobacco is as much a staple along the Ontario shore of Lake Erie as in the Kentucky pennyroyal; and the growing of rice and cotton in California has not prevented Los Angeles from being in a sense the capital of Iowa. On the other hand the rise of mill towns in the Carolina piedmont and the growth of manufacturing at Richmond and Birmingham have not made these Northern. It may be admitted, however, that Miami, Palm Beach, and Coral Gables are Southern only in latitude. They were vacant wastes until Flagler, Fifth Avenue, and the realtors discovered and subdivided them.

The South has never had a focus. New York has plied as much of its trade as Baltimore or New Orleans; and White Sulphur Springs did not quite eclipse all other mountain and coast resorts for vacation patronage. The lack of a metropolis was lamented in 1857 by an advocate of Southern independence,[1] as an essential for shaping and radiating a coherent philosophy to fit the prevailing conditions of life. But without a consolidating press or pulpit or other definite apparatus the South has maintained a considerable solidarity through thick and thin, through peace and war and peace again. What is its essence? Not state rights — Calhoun himself was for years a nationalist, and some advocates of independence hoped for a complete merging of the several states into a unitary Southern republic; not free trade — sugar and hemp growers have ever been protectionists; not slavery — in the eighteenth century this was of conti-

1 *Russell's Magazine* (Charleston), I. 106.

From the *American Historical Review*, 34 (October, 1928), 30–43, by permission of the editors.

nental legality, and in the twentieth it is legal nowhere; not Democracy – there were many Federalists in Washington's day and many Whigs in Clay's; not party predominance by any name, for Virginia, Georgia, and Mississippi were "doubtful states" from Jackson's time to Buchanan's. It is not the land of cotton alone or of plantations alone; and it has not always been the land of "Dixie," for before its ecstatic adoption in 1861 that spine-tingling tune was a mere "walk around" of Christie's minstrels. Yet it is a land with a unity despite its diversity, with a people having common joys and common sorrows, and, above all, as to the white folk a people with a common resolve indomitably maintained – that it shall be and remain a white man's country. The consciousness of a function in these premises, whether expressed with the frenzy of a demagogue or maintained with a patrician's quietude, is the cardinal test of a Southerner and the central theme of Southern history.

It arose as soon as the negroes became numerous enough to create a problem of race control in the interest of orderly government and the maintenance of Caucasian civilization. Slavery was instituted not merely to provide control of labor but also as a system of racial adjustment and social order. And when in the course of time slavery was attacked, it was defended not only as a vested interest, but with vigor and vehemence as a guarantee of white supremacy and civilization. Its defenders did not always take pains to say that this was what they chiefly meant, but it may nearly always be read between their lines, and their hearers and readers understood it without overt expression.[2] Otherwise it would be impossible to account for the fervid secessionism of many non-slaveholders and the eager service of thousands in the Confederate army.

The non-slaveholders of course were diverse in their conditions and sentiments. Those in the mountains and the deep pine woods were insulated to such degree that public opinion hardly existed, and they chose between alternatives only when issues created in other quarters were forced upon them. Those in the black belts, on the other hand, had their lives conditioned by the presence of the negroes; and they had apparatus of court days, militia musters, and political barbecues as well as neighborhood conversation to keep them abreast of affairs. A mechanic of Iuka, Mississippi, wrote in the summer of 1861: "I am a Georgian raised I am Forty years Old A tinner By Trade I Raised the First Confederate Flag that I Ever Heard Of that was in 1851 in the Town of Macon Miss. Notwithstanding the Many Radicules I Encounter'd I Told the Citizens that they would All Be Glad to Rally under Such a Flag Some Day which is at present true."[3] This personal tale was told to prove his title to a voice in Confederate policy. His main theme was a demand that the permanent Confederate constitution exclude negroes from all employment except agricultural labor and do-

2 Many expressions were explicit, for example, the remarks of Mr. Standard at Richmond in 1829: "The property we seek to protect . . . is not mere brute matter . . . but it consists of intelligent, sentient, responsible beings, that have passions to be inflamed, hearts to feel, understandings to be enlightened, and who are capable of catching the flame of enthusiasm from the eloquent effusions of agitators . . . ; and who may not only be lost to their masters as property, but may change conditions and become masters themselves, so far at least as the ravages of a servile war shall have [error for leave] any subject to be ruled over." *Proceedings and Debates of the Virginia State Convention of 1829–30* (Richmond, 1830), p. 306.

3 Manuscript letter in private possession.

mestic service in order that the handicrafts be reserved for white artisans like himself.

The overseer of a sugar estate forty miles below New Orleans inscribed a prayer on the plantation journal:

Thursday 13 June 1861
This Day is set a part By presedent Jefferson Davis for fasting and praying owing to the Deplorable condition ower southern country is In My Prayer Sincerely to God is that every Black Republican in the Hole combined whorl either man woman o chile that is opposed to negro slavery as it existed in the Southern confederacy shal be trubled with pestilents and calamitys of all Kinds and Drag out the Balance of there existance in Misray and Degradation with scarsely food and rayment enughf to keep sole and Body to gather and o God I pray the to Direct a bullet or a bayonet to pirce The Hart of every northern soldier that invades southern soile and after the Body has rendered up its traterish sole gave it a trators reward a Birth In the Lake of Fires and Brimstone my honest convicksion is that every man wome and chile that has gave aide to the abolishionist are fit subjects for Hell I all so ask the to aide the southern Confederacy in maintaining ower rites and establishing the confederate Government Believing this case the prares from the wicked will prevaileth much Amen[4]

This overseer's pencilled prayer is the most rampant fire-eating expression which I have encountered in any quarter. He and the tinner had an economic interest in the maintenance of slavery, the one to assure the presence of laborers for him to boss, the other to restrain competition in his trade. But both of them, and a million of their non-slaveholding like, had a still stronger social prompting: the white men's ways must prevail; the negroes must be kept innocuous.

In the 'forties when most of the planters were Whig some of the Democratic politicians thought it strange that their own party should be the more energetic in defense of slavery; and in 1860 they were perhaps puzzled again that the Bell and Everett Constitutional Union ticket drew its main support from among the slaveholders. The reason for this apparent anomaly lay doubtless in the two facts, that men of wealth had more to lose in any cataclysm, and that masters had less antipathy to negroes than non-slaveholders did. In daily contact with blacks from birth, and often on a friendly basis of patron and retainer, the planters were in a sort of partnership with their slaves, reckoning upon their good-will or at least possessing a sense of security as a fruit of long habituation to fairly serene conditions. But the white toilers lived outside this partnership and suffered somewhat from its competition. H. R. Helper in his *Impending Crisis* (1857) urged them to wreck the system by destroying slavery; and when this had been accomplished without their aid he vented in his fantastic *Nojoque* (1867) a spleen against the negroes, advocating their expulsion from the United States as a preliminary to their universal extermination. Thus he called for class war upon a double front, to humble the "lords of the lash" and then to destroy the "black and bi-colored caitiffs" who cumbered the white man's world. By his alliterative rhetoric and shrewdly selected statistics Helper captured some Northern propagandists and the historians whom they begat, but if he made any converts among Southern yeomen they are not of record. His notions had come to him

[4] When I made this transcript twenty years ago the manuscript journal was on Magnolia plantation in Plaquemines Parish, Louisiana. The item is in the handwriting of J. A. Randall, overseer.

during residence in California and the North; they were therefore to be taken skeptically. His programmes repudiated humane tradition, disregarded vital actualities, and evoked Northern aid to make over the South in its own image. These things, and perhaps the last especially, were not to be sanctioned. In fact, for reasons common in the world at large, the Southern whites were not to be divided into sharply antagonistic classes. Robert J. Walker said quite soundly in 1856:

> In all the slave States there is a large majority of voters who are non-slaveholders; but they are devoted to the institutions of the South – they would defend them with their lives – and on this question the South are [*sic*] a united people. The class, composed of many small farmers, of merchants, professional men, mechanics, overseers, and other industrial classes, constitute mainly the patrol of the South, and cheerfully unite in carrying out those laws essential to preserve the institution. Against a powerful minority and constant agitation slavery could not exist in any State.[5]

He wrote this to explain the poor prospect of slavery in Kansas; he might have used the same phrasing to explain its persistence in Delaware or Missouri. Habitat grouping, it is clear, had a cementing force great enough to overcome the cleaving tendency of economic stratification. So strong was it, indeed, that sundry free negroes gave warm endorsement to the project of Southern independence.[6]

It is perhaps less fruitful to seek the social classes at large which were warm and those which were cool toward independence than to inquire why the citizens of certain areas were prevailingly ardent while those in another zone were indifferent or opposed, why for example the whole tier from South Carolina to Texas seceded spontaneously but no other states joined them until after Lincoln's call for troops. The reason lay in preceding history as well as in current conditions. The economic factor of the cotton belt's interest in free trade and its recurrent chagrin at protective tariff enactments is by no means negligible. The rancor produced by nullification and the "force bill" had been revived in South Carolina by the repeal of the compromise tariff in 1842, and it did not then die. The quarrels of Georgia with the federal authorities over Indian lands, with Alabama and Mississippi looking on in interested sympathy, were contributing episodes to make the lower South alert; and the heavy negro proportions in their black belts, together with immaturity in the social order, made their people more sensitive than those of Virginia to the menace of disturbance from outside.

Slavery questions, which had never been quite negligible since the framing of the Constitution, gained a febrile activity from the abolition agitation; and the study of Congressional mathematics focussed the main attention upon the rivalry of the sections in territorial enlargement. The North had control of the lower house, as recurrent votes on the Wilmot Proviso showed; and California's admission upset the sectional equilibrium in the Senate. For Yancey, Rhett, and Quitman and for the pamphleteers Longstreet, Bryan, and Trescot, this was enough. The North now had the strength of a giant; the South should strike for independence before that strength should grow yet greater and be consolidated for crushing purposes. But the gestures of

5 *DeBow's Review*, XXI. 591–592.

6 U. B. Phillips, *American Negro Slavery*, p. 436; R. H. Williams, *With the Border Ruffians* (London, 1908), p. 441.

Cass, Webster, and Fillmore gave ground for hope that the giant would not use his power against Southern home rule, and the crisis was deferred. Southern friends and foes of the Compromise of 1850 were alert thenceforward for tokens of Northern will. Events through the ensuing decade, somewhat assisted by the fire-eaters and culminating in a Republican's election to the Presidency, converted a new multitude to the shibboleth: "The alternative: a separate nationality or the Africanization of the South."[7]

Walter Lippmann has analyzed political process in general as if he had our present study specifically in mind:

> Since the general opinions of large numbers of persons are almost certain to be a vague and confusing medley, action cannot be taken until those opinions have been factored down, canalized, compressed and made uniform. The making of one general will out of a multitude of general wishes . . . consists essentially in the use of symbols which assemble emotions after they have been detached from their ideas. . . . The process, therefore, by which general opinions are brought to co-operation consists in an intensification of feeling and a degradation of significance.[8]

The tension of 1850 had brought much achievement in this direction. "Southern rights" had come to mean racial security, self-determination by the whites whether in or out of the Union, and all things ancillary to the assured possession of these. Furthermore a programme had been framed to utilize state sovereignty whether to safeguard the South as a minority within the Union or to legitimate its exit into national independence.

The resurgence of these notions and emotions after their abeyance in 1851 need not be traced in detail. Suffice it to say that legal sanction for the spread of slaveholding, regardless of geographical potentialities, became the touchstone of Southern rights; and the rapid rise of the Republican party which denied this sanction, equally regardless of geographical potentialities, tipped the balance in lower Southern policy. Many were primed in 1856 for a stroke in case Frémont should be elected that year; and though he fell short of an electoral majority, the strength shown by his ticket increased the zeal of South-savers through the next quadrennium. The so-called Southern commercial conventions became a forum and *DeBow's Review* an organ for the airing of projects, mad or sane, for annexing Cuba, promoting direct trade with Europe, boycotting Northern manufactures and Northern colleges, procuring Southern text-books for Southern schools, reopening the African slave trade — anything and everything which might agitate and perhaps consolidate the South in a sense of bafflement within the Union and a feeling of separate destiny. Many clergymen gave their aid, particularly by praising slavery as a biblical and benevolent institution.

Pierre Soulé tried in 1857, as Calhoun had done eight years before, to create a Southern party separate from the Democrats;[9] and next year Yancey launched his League of United Southerners. Ere long a rural editor blurted what many must have been thinking:

> That the North sectionalized will acquire possession of this Government at no distant day we look upon as no longer a matter of doubt. . . . It is inevitable. The South — the

[7] The title of a pamphlet by William H. Holcombe, M.D. (New Orleans, 1860).

[8] *The Phantom Public* (New York, 1925), p. 47.

[9] New Orleans *Crescent*, June 17, 1857.

whole South even — cannot avert it. We may determine to fight the battle with our foes within the Union, . . . but we will fight only to be defeated. The Union of the South is indeed of great moment — not however for successful resistance in this Union, but for going out of it under circumstances the most favorable to the speedy formation of a separate and independent government.[10]

Various expressions in Northern papers, debates in Congress, and events in Kansas and elsewhere had fanned these flames when the stroke of John Brown fell upon Harper's Ferry. This event was taken as a demonstration that abolitionists had lied in saying they were concerned with moral suasion only, and it stimulated suspicion that Republicans were abolitionists in disguise. In December the South Carolina legislature when expressing sympathy with Virginia intimated that she was ripe for secession and invited all Southern states to meet in convention at once to concert measures for united action. In February the Alabama legislature asserted that under no circumstances would the commonwealth submit to "the foul domination of a sectional Northern party," and it instructed the governor in the event of a Republican's election to the Presidency to order the election of delegates to a convention of the state to consider and do whatever in its judgment her rights, interest, and honor might require.

There was little to do in the interim but discuss principles and portents and to jockey the situation slightly to prepare for the crisis or try to prevent it according to what individuals might think best. In an editorial of January 9, 1860, on "The true position of the South: Not aggrandisement but safety," the New Orleans *Crescent,* which was long an advocate of moderation, said:

The South does not claim the right of controlling the North in the choice of a President; she admits fully and explicitly that the Northern people possess the prerogative of voting as they please. But at the same time the South asserts that while the North holds the legal right of casting her voice as to her may seem best, she has no *moral* right to so cast it as to effect the ruin of the South; and if she does so cast it, in full view of its injurious effects upon us, . . . she, in effect, commits an act of covert hostility upon us that will render it impossible for us to live longer in intimate relations.

On April 15, the *Delta,* replying to a recent lecture at New Orleans by George D. Prentice of Louisville, denied that Clay and Webster, "those demiurgic heroes of his political faith," could have sufficed for the present occasion:

The period of mere political formation is past, and the period for the solution of great social and industrial problems is at hand. Mere constitutional lore here can do nothing; mere skill in adjusting balances of political power can do nothing. Is it just to hold the negro in bondage? Is negro slavery inimical to the rights of white men? Is it best for both the white and black man — best for the interests of agriculture, best for the needs of commerce and useful arts, and best for social stability and civilization? These and kindred questions imperiously demand to be answered, and they are precisely the questions which the old school of statesmen strenuously refused to look in the face. . . . The truth is, we are in the midst of facts having a philosophy of their own which we must master for ourselves, leaving dead men to take care of the dead past. The Sphinx which is now propounding its riddles to us the dead knew nothing about; consequently

[10] *The Southron* (Orangeburg, S. C.), quoted in the *Southern Guardian* (Columbia, S. C.), May 20, 1859.

no voice from the grave can tell us how to get rid of the monster.

After the nominating conventions had put four tickets in the field the newspapers began a running debate upon the relative merits of Douglas, Breckinridge, and Bell for Southern purposes and the degree of menace in the Lincoln candidacy. The Natchez *Free Trader*, which until June 27 mastheaded the names of Albert G. Brown and Fernando Wood, accepted next day the Richmond nominations:

We hoist today the flag of the Union-saving National Democratic nominees, Breckinridge and Lane, *sans peur et sans reproche*. With records so fair that none can attack them, they will win the hearts of all the people of the land, be elected by a vote so flattering as to cause the hearts of the noblest and best to beat with honest exaltation and pride, and so administer the Government as to have the blessings of the people showered on them and elicit the unrestrained admiration of an enlightened world.

Such bombast as this might survive the summer; but when the October elections brought a virtual certainty of Lincoln's election the discussion took another phase. The friends of each minor ticket demanded that the other two be withdrawn or forsaken. Douglas and Bell men agreed at least that Breckinridge ought to be abandoned. The Nashville *Union and American*, in reply on October 16 to such a demand from the Nashville *Patriot*, said that Breckinridge might still be elected by Southern concentration upon him, "in as much as it will prove to the North that we are determined to have our rights." And as a last appeal, November 6, the New Orleans *Delta* said, urging votes for Breckinridge as against Bell or Douglas:

Is this the time to indorse the representatives of a half-way, compromising, submissive policy? When the whole North is sectional shall the South be national, when nationality can mean nothing but an acquiescence in the employment of national means to accomplish sectional purposes? Never before in the history of any free and brave people was so bold a challenge as that which the North now throws at us received in any other way than the stern and proud defiance of a united and determined community.

Among the Bell organs the New Orleans *Bee* gave a remarkably sound analysis in an editorial of July 27: "The restlessness of the South touching the agitation of the slavery question arises rather from the apprehension of what the aggressive policy of the North may hereafter effect, than from what it has already accomplished. For . . . we may safely affirm that thus far no practical injury has resulted." The Southern failure in colonizing Kansas, it continued, was not a grievance, for: "prudent and far-seeing men predicted the utter impracticability of carrying the design into execution. . . . Slavery will go where it will pay. No slaveholder for the sake of an abstraction will amuse himself by earning five per cent in Kansas on the labor of his chattels, when with absolutely less toil it will give him fifteen per cent in the cotton or sugar fields of Louisiana." On its own score the *Bee* concluded: "We apprehend that the Black Republicans are dogs whose bark is more dangerous than their bite. The South is too precious to the North to be driven out of the Union." Its colleague the *Crescent* expressed a belief as late as October 20, that if the Republican party should win the contest, its "unnatural and feverish vitality" would reach exhaustion within a year or two. In the United States thus far, the

Crescent argued, parties had arisen and fallen in rapid succession.

> But all of these parties were national. The principles they advocated were of common application to the whole country, and their members and adherents were found in every quarter and every State of the Union. If these parties were temporary and short-lived in their character and constitution, still more so must the Black Republican party be, sectional as it is in its organization and principles, and obnoxious to a deeper hatred and more bitter opposition than any other organization that has yet made its appearance in the political arena. It is impossible that such a party can long exist.

Just before election day George Fitzhugh of Virginia wrote to the Charleston *Mercury* a long letter concluding: "In the Union there is no hope for us. Let us gather courage from despair, and quit the Union." The editor when printing this, November 9, remarked: "Mr. Fitzhugh is a little excitable. We intend to 'quit the Union,' but without any 'despair' whatever. We'll quit it with a round hip! hip! hurrah!!"

But now that the partizans of Breckinridge, Bell, and Douglas had met a common defeat, their lines were broken with regard to the Southern recourse. Some of the Breckinridge men opposed secession unless and until the Lincoln government should commit an "overt act" of injury, but many supporters of Bell and Douglas turned to the policy of prompt strokes.[11] The New Orleans *Crescent* and *Bee* are again clear exponents. On November 8 the *Crescent* said: "We read the result in the face of every citizen upon the street. There is an universal feeling that an insult has been deliberately tendered our people, which is responded to not by noisy threats or passionate objurgations, but a settled determination that the South shall never be oppressed under Mr. Lincoln's administration." But it cherished a shadowy hope that electors chosen on the Republican ticket might yet refrain from putting "a sectional President in the chair of Washington!" On December 17 the *Bee* admitted that it had yielded to the prodigious tide of public sentiment, and said in explanation: "It was evident indeed, that amid all the lip service professed for the Union there had dwelt in the hearts of Southerners a tacit determination to regard the election of Lincoln as proof of a settled and immutable policy of aggression by the North toward the South, and to refuse further political affiliation with those who by that act should declare themselves our enemies." On the following January 3 the *Crescent* said:

> It is by secession alone that we [Louisiana] can be placed in close affinity with all of our sisters of the Gulf and South Atlantic seaboard, who have given guarantees . . . that they will be out of the Union long in advance of our action and ready to receive us in the Government that shall have been established.[12] South Carolina, Georgia, Mississippi, Florida, Alabama, Louisiana, and

11 Unionism among many of the Bell supporters had been conditioned from the first, almost explicitly, upon constitutionalism as interpreted in favor of Southern rights. For example the convention in Georgia which responded to the call for organizing the party and sent delegates to Baltimore adopted a platform asserting that slavery was established in the Constitution, that the territories were the property of the states jointly, that Congress and the territorial legislatures were alike incapable of impairing the right of slave property, and that it was the duty of Congress to protect the rights of slaveholders in the territories. *Southern Recorder* (Milledgeville, Ga.), May 8, 1860.

12 These pledges had been conveyed by commissioners appointed by the governors of sundry commonwealths to convey to the governors, legislatures, and conventions of other states assur-

Texas are knit by God and their own hearts indissolubly together. . . .

Believe not that any State has the right to expect another to await her action in an emergency like this. *We have as much right to complain of the tardiness of the border States as they have of our haste.* . . . A people who wait for others to aid them in vindicating their rights are already enslaved, for now, as in every other period of history —

"In native swords and native ranks
The only hope of freedom dwells."

The upper South had votaries of independence no less outspoken than those of the cotton belt, but they were too few to carry their states prior to a Northern "overt act." Arguments and eloquence by visiting commissioners might sway the minds and thrill the hearts of delegates, but none of these conventions took a decisive step until Lincoln's call for troops. Indeed there was a project of organizing the border states for a course of their own, even to the extreme of a central confederacy separate alike from the "Black Republican" North and the "hotspur" South. When this was pinched out, the sequel showed that the boundary of predominant Southern loyalty was not Mason and Dixon's line but a curving zone seldom touching that landmark.

Many Virginians, perhaps most of them, sanctioned the change of allegiance reluctantly; and some, chiefly in the Wheeling panhandle, revolted sharply against it. On the other hand the course of the Federal government during the war and after its close alienated so many borderers that in a sense Kentucky joined the Confederacy after the war was over.

While the war dragged its disheartening length and the hopes of independence faded, queries were raised in some Southern quarters as to whether yielding might not be the wiser course. Lincoln in his plan of reconstruction had shown unexpected magnanimity; the Republican party, discarding that obnoxious name, had officially styled itself merely Unionist; and the Northern Democrats, although outvoted, were still a friendly force to be reckoned upon. Die-hard statesmen and loyal soldiers carried on till the collapse. The governors in the "late so-called Confederate States" were now ready with soft speeches, but the Federal soldiery clapped them into prison until Andrew Johnson relaxed from his brief punitive phase.

With Johnson then on Lincoln's path "back to normalcy," Southern hearts were lightened only to sink again when radicals in Congress, calling themselves Republicans once more, overslaughed the Presidential programme and set events in train which seemed to make "the Africanization of the South" inescapable. To most of the whites, doubtless, the prospect showed no gleam of hope.

But Edward A. Pollard, a Virginia critic of Davis, chronicler of the war and bewailer of the "lost cause," took courage in 1868 to write his most significant book, *The Lost Cause Regained.* The folly of politicians, he said, had made the South defend slavery seemingly "as a property tenure, or as a peculiar institution of labour; when the true ground of defence was as of a barrier against a contention and war of races."[13] The pro-slavery claims on the basis of constitutional right he denounced in retrospect as flimsily technical and utterly futile in the face of a steadily encroaching moral sentiment; and the stroke for independence in the name of liberty he thought as fallacious

ances of secession as soon as the procedure could be completed and invitations for union in a new nation or confederacy. . . .

13 E. A. Pollard, *The Lost Cause Regained* (New York, 1868), p. 13.

as the later expectation of generosity which had brought the Confederate collapse.[14]

It has been curiously reserved for the South to obtain *after* the war the actual experience of oppression, and of that measure of despotism which would have amply justified the commencement of hostilities. If it fought, in 1860, for principles too abstract, it has superabundant causes for rebellion now, which although they may not, and need not produce another war, yet have the effect to justify, in a remarkable way, the first appeal to arms.[15]

In elaboration of this: "The black thread of the Negro has been spun throughout the scheme of Reconstruction. A design is betrayed to give to him the political control of the South, not so much as a benefit to him, . . . as to secure power to the Republican party."[16]

But in the defeats of proposals for negro suffrage in seven states from Connecticut to Colorado, and particularly in the ovation with which the Philadelphia convention of 1866 had received a resolution urging the Southern whites not to submit to negro rule, he saw promise of effective support and eventual success in undoing Reconstruction.[17] Therefore:

Let us come back to the true hope of the South. It is to enter bravely with new allies and new auspices the contest for the supremacy of the white man, and with it the preservation of the dearest political traditions of the country. "WHITE" is the winning word, says a North Carolina paper, and let us never be done repeating it. . . . It is the irresistible sympathy of races, which will not, cannot fail. . . . It is this instinct which the South will at last summon to her aid, when her extremity demands it.[18]

Before the farther bank of the slough of despond was fully attained, the question was raised as to the path beyond. In a remarkable address in 1875 Wiley P. Harris of Mississippi lamented the political exploitation of the negroes: "The mass of them don't vote, but are literally voted. They are ridden and driven by a little nest of men who are alien to the state in feeling. . . . The result is a government at once imperious and contemptible, a tyranny at once loathsome and deadly." He bade the carpet-baggers farewell in advance of their going: "I assure these men that their last card has been played, and it has not won. This trumpery no longer deceives anybody, and it matters not which party prevails in 1876, no national administration will again incur the odium of propping them up." But with merely restoring white local domination he would not be content. Appealing specifically for a renewed and permanent union of Democrats with liberal Republicans throughout the country, he said:

To reconcile and nationalize the South, to lead it out of the cul de sac of sectionalism into the broad stream of national life, . . . to restore peace, good will and confidence between the members of this great family of States, will lay the solid and durable foundation of a party which will surely win and long retain the hearts of the American people. . . . For one, I long to see a government at Washington, and a government here, toward which I can feel a genuine sentiment of reverence and respect. It is a dreary life we lead here, with a national government ever suspicious and ever frowning, and a home government feeble, furtive, false and fraudulent. Under such influences

[14] *Ibid.*, pp. 20, 50, 116.

[15] *Ibid.*, pp. 51–52.

[16] *Ibid.*, p. 129.

[17] *Ibid.*, pp. 133, 162.

[18] *Ibid.*, p. 165.

the feeling of patriotism must die out amongst us, and this will accomplish the ruin of a noble population. . . . We are in a new world. We are moving on a new plane. It is better that we hang a millstone about our necks than cling to these old issues. To cling to them is to perpetuate sectional seclusion.[19]

Lamar's eulogy of Sumner and the speeches and editorials of Grady were much to the same effect, and likewise were the efforts of other broadminded men. But a certain sense of bafflement and of defensive self-containment persists to our own day, because the negro population remains as at least a symbolic potentiality. Virtually all respectable whites had entered the Democratic ranks in the later 'sixties to combat *à outrance* the Republican programme of negro incitement. A dozen years sufficed to restore white control, whereupon they began to differ among themselves upon various issues. Many joined the People's party; and in some quarters a fusion was arranged of Populists and Republicans to carry elections. In the stress of campaigning this threatened to bring from within the South a stimulus to negroes as political auxiliaries.

But by Southern hypothesis, exalted into a creed, negroes in the mass were incompetent for any good political purpose and by reason of their inexperience and racial unwisdom were likely to prove subversive. To remove the temptation to white politicians to lead negroes to the polls again, "white primaries" were instituted to control nominations, educational requirements for the suffrage were inserted in the state constitutions, and the Bryanizing of the Democratic party was accepted as a means of healing a white rift. Even these devices did not wholly lay the spectre of "negro domination"; for the fifteenth amendment stood in the Constitution and the calendar of Congress was not yet free of "force bills." For every Lodge and Foraker there arose a Tillman and a Vardaman, with a Watson and a Blease to spare.

The sentiments and symbols have not been wholly divorced from reason. When California whites made extravagant demands in fear that her three per cent. of Japanese might increase to four and capture the business of "The Coast," Congress responded as if it were an appendage of the state legislature. But white Southerners when facing problems real or fancied concerning the ten million negroes in their midst can look to the federal authorities for no more at best than a tacit acquiescence in what their state governments may do. Acquiescence does not evoke enthusiasm; and until an issue shall arise predominant over the lingering one of race, political solidarity at the price of provincial status is maintained to keep assurance doubly, trebly sure that the South shall remain "a white man's country."

[19] Speech of W. P. Harris at a Democratic campaign meeting, Jackson, Miss., Aug. 23, 1875. Lowry and McCardle, *History of Mississippi*, pp. 396–400.

Russel B. Nye:

THE SLAVE POWER CONSPIRACY: 1830–1860

THE keynote of the abolitionist histories of the antebellum period, and of the literature produced by the abolitionist movement, was the thesis that the fight against slavery was not only a struggle to free the Negro from bondage, but one to remove as a dominant force in American life the threat of a well-organized, aggressive, threatening "Slave Power conspiracy," or what is called "Slaveocracy." For the abolitionists, who remained a minority in the North throughout the entire pre-war period, the "Slave Power threat" served as an invaluable device in gaining public support. There was, they charged, a tacit secret agreement among Southern slaveholders not only to maintain undisturbed their "peculiar institution," but to foist it on the nation by extending it to the territories and free states (possibly to whites), to destroy civil liberties, control the policies of the Federal government, and complete the formation of a nation-wide ruling aristocracy based on a slave economy.[1]

To many in the North who were relatively uninterested in the Negro's freedom, the appeal of the charge was strong. Mechanics, immigrant laborers, farmers and lower- and middle-class workmen, prone to suspect the motives of the rich and powerful, found in the abolitionist contention more logic than is usually supposed. During the thirties the abolitionists warned constantly of the existence of such a conspiratorial movement to crush liberty, though the term "Slave Power" did not come into wide use until the fifties. In 1839 the National Convention of Abolitionists, meeting at Albany, resolved that "the events of the last five or six years leave no room for doubt that the SLAVE POWER is now waging a deliberate and determined war against the liberties of the free states,"[2] and by 1845 repetitions of the charge became common. From that date on Northern opinion was subjected to an increasing barrage of proof, and began to be colored appreciably by acceptance of it.[3] As the fear of "black Republican-

1 For definitive historical treatments from the abolitionist point of view, see Henry Wilson, *The History of the Rise and Fall of the Slave Power in America* (Boston and New York, 1872), and J. E. Cairnes, *The Slave Power* (2nd ed., New York, 1863). The most extreme indictment is that of John S. Dye, *History of the Plots and Crimes of the Great Conspiracy to Overthrow Liberty in America* (New York, 1866), which accuses slaveholders of poisoning Harrison and Tyler and attempting to assassinate Jackson.

2 The Cincinnati *Philanthropist*, September 17, 1839. See also *The Proceedings of the Rhode Island Antislavery Convention . . .* (Providence, 1836), *The Philanthropist*, June 7, 1837, and *The Emancipator*, February 6, 1838.

3 Repetitions of the charge are too numerous to list, but samples may be found in the Utica, N. Y., *Friend of Man*, September 2, 1840; *The Massachusetts Abolitionist*, February 6, 1840; *The Liberator*, May 20, 27, and June 3, 1842; J. Q.

From *Science and Society*, 10 (Summer, 1946), 262–274, by permission of the publisher.

ism" and miscegenation was used by the pro-slavery element to unify Southern opinion, so the genuine threat of the Slave Power became an important factor in consolidating anti-slavery sentiment in the North.

What was the Slave Power of which the abolitionist warned, and from what conditions did it arise? A typical definition called it "that control in and over the government which is exercised by a comparatively small number of persons . . . bound together in a common interest, by being owners of slaves"; all definitions agreed that it was fundamentally "an aristocracy constituted and organized on the basis of ownership of slaves."[4] Its origins lay in the institution of slavery, which "developed and gratified the most intense spirit of personal pride, a love of class distinctions, and the lust of dominion. Hence arose a commanding power, ever sensitive, jealous, proscriptive, dominating, and aggressive. . . ."[5] The threat of Slave Power domination was intensified, said the abolitionists, by the danger of a coalition of Southern slaveholder and Northern capitalist to form a ruling oligarchy. The two had certain moral affinities and a clear identity of interest, it was pointed out, and concerted action was logical and imminent.[6] The tendency to include in the term "Slave Power" not only slaveholders but also Northern industrialists grew, until by 1850 the term meant, as Wendell Phillips strikingly phrased it, an alliance of "the Lords of the Lash and the Lords of the Loom." "The wealth of the North and the wealth of the South," cried *The Antislavery Bugle*, "are combined to crush the liberal, free, progressive spirit of the age," and the fight against the Slave Power became a battle against conservatism, reaction, aristocracy, and the power of capital – in Ohio and Massachusetts as well as in South Carolina.[7]

It was not difficult for the abolitionists to recruit evidence to prove that there actually was a Slave Power conspiracy. After 1850, when they began to publicize the charge in earnest, they interpreted the drift of recent events in the light of its existence. Joshua Giddings of Ohio, writing in the forties, listed ten proofs from history to substantiate the belief that a well-organized Southern slaveholding cabal had operated in the past, and might again: the fugitive slave law of 1793, the Creek-Negro troubles in Florida in 1815; the Seminole War, the maintenance of slavery in the District of Columbia, the controversy over the mails and petitions in Congress in 1836, attacks on free speech and press, and demands for the extension of slavery to the Southwest and for the reopening of the slave trade. Seward in 1855 added the Missouri Compromise, the annexation of

Adams in *The Antislavery Bugle*, March 10, 1848; J. G. Palfry, *Papers on the Slave Power* (Boston, 1846); Joshua Giddings, *Speeches in Congress* (Cleveland, 1853), etc. Wilson, *op. cit.*, II, p. 189, fixed the beginning of the Mexican War as the date of the general acceptance of the belief.

[4] Anon., *Five Years' Progress of the Slave Power* (Boston, 1852), p. 2, and *Facts for the People* (February 1, 1856). See also Gamaliel Bailey, the Cincinnati *Weekly Herald and Philanthropist*, September 16, 1844.

[5] Henry Wilson, *op. cit.*, I, p. 2. See also William Goodell's analysis, "The Philosophy of the Slaveholding Supremacy," *The American Jubilee*, January and March, 1855.

[6] Gamaliel Bailey, *The Philanthropist*, January 22, 1839; Garrison, *The Liberator*, October 23, 1840; Cassius Clay, *The Antislavery Bugle*, July 5, 1851.

[7] Phillips, speech to the American Antislavery Society, *The National Antislavery Standard*, June 14, 1859, and Bailey, *The Antislavery Bugle*, November 9, 1850. See also "The Alliance with the Northern Money Power," *Five Years' Progress of the Slave Power*, p. 25–31.

Texas, the Mexican War, the Kansas struggle, and the 1850 Compromise to the list of Slave Power victories.[8] The Dred Scott case clinched the evidence, and by 1858 a substantial number of Northerners were ready to believe, as did the non-abolitionist Cincinnati *Daily Commercial* of March 12, 1857, that "There is such a thing as the SLAVE POWER. It has marched over and annihilated the boundaries of the states. We are now one great homogeneous slaveholding community." The aim of this conspiracy, whose existence was thus established, was threefold: to reopen the slave trade; to extend slavery throughout the entire nation and beyond; and, most dangerous threat of all, to make the free white man a virtual slave to a privileged aristocracy of Southern slaveholder and Northern capitalist.[9]

Southern agitation after 1850 for the renewal of the slave trade lent rather convincing proof to the first claim. The failing slave economy led many Southerners to advocate a revival of slave importations as the only remedy for the South's economic difficulties, and abolitionists seized upon the argument as evidence that the Slave Power intended to entrench itself even more firmly by thus bolstering the institution upon which it rested. In the years following, Southern demands became more insistent and frequent (a marked illustration of how completely the South had become committed to the defense and maintenance of slavery) while the abolitionist press kept careful watch of ruses, such as proposals to import "indentured" Negroes, Negro apprentices, or to form "African Labor Importation Associations." The loosening of the 1808 laws against the slave trade or their repeal, warned the abolitionists, would result without doubt in a new and doubly potent Slave Power.[10]

Stressed more strongly by the abolitionists and supported by more substantial evidence was the claim that the Slave Power intended to establish slavery on a nationwide and possibly a hemispheric basis. Gamaliel Bailey in 1844 exposed "a deliberate plot . . . to sustain the slavery of this country . . . and to extend it over almost illimitable regions," and for more than a decade the press reported a boast by Toombs of Georgia that he would some day call the roll of his slaves on Bunker Hill.[11] Furthermore, the abolitionist could cite the Kansas troubles, the attacks on anti-slavery men in the North, the Mexican War, Texas, the various Congressional compromises, the argument over slavery in the territories, and a host of other proofs. Nor was the Slave Power innocent of designs on Central America. It intended to make slave states of New Mexico and Utah, divide California into a free and a slave state, split Texas into four new slave states, take over at least Mexico, Cuba, San Domingo, Yucatan, and Nicaragua,

8 J. R. Giddings, *The Rights of Free States Subverted* (n. p., 1844), and Seward's Albany speech, in *Facts for the People,* November 1, 1855. See also the detailed analysis in *Facts for the People,* February 1, March 1, and April 11, 1856.

9 The most sweeping indictment is that of chapter 4, "Preparation for Future Movement," *Five Years' Progress of the Slave Power.*

10 *The Antislavery Bugle* for May 16, 1857, February 27 and March 27, 1858; *The Radical Abolitionist,* April, 1858; *The National Era,* March 10, April 1 and 10, 1859; *The American Jubilee,* February, 1855; and *The Emancipator and Free American,* March 16, 1853, contain typical warnings.

11 The Cincinnati *Weekly Herald and Philanthropist,* May 7, 1844; *The National Era,* August 23, 1855; *The Antislavery Bugle,* September 15, 1855; *Facts for the People,* September, 1855; *The National Antislavery Standard,* December 20, 1856. An especially detailed analysis in "The Plan and the Object," *The National Era,* February 22, 1849.

"consolidating the whole into a vast slave empire."[12] Toward the close of the fifties the accusation formed a major portion of almost every abolition argument, until anti-extension became, by way of the Republican party, a cardinal political principle in the North.

More difficult to establish, but tremendously effective as a propaganda issue, was the accusation that the Slave Power aimed eventually to subvert the liberties of white men, and to introduce virtual white slavery as national policy. Since slavery, reasoned the abolitionists, was founded upon a violation of the principles of liberty and free government, it followed that by the simple fact of its existence slavery was a constant threat to those principles.[13] Abolitionists had warned from the beginning that the Slave Power would some day crush white rights as it had black, and after 1845 the warnings became clearer and more frequent.[14] For proof of their charges the abolitionists had but to turn to the arguments in support of slavery advanced by the slaveholders themselves, particularly to the "positive good" school of thought developed in the South after 1835, a new philosophy of bondage which boldly asserted slavery to be a beneficial institution, the single sure foundation for society, church, and state, while freedom was asserted to be a danger to the human race.[15] Certain aspects of this pro-slavery argument lent themselves admirably to the abolitionist contention.

Slavery, said many in the South, had natural, historical, and moral justification. Governor McDuffie of South Carolina believed that the examination of any community showed that "servitude, in some form, is one of its essential constituents"; Calhoun called slavery "a universal condition," and Chancellor Harper thought that "it is as much the order of nature that men should enslave each other as that animals should prey upon each other."[16] At the same time, proslavery men accused free society of dismal failure. It was, said the New Orleans *Delta*, ". . . radically wrong and rotten. It is self-destroying, and can never exist happily or normally, unless it is qualified by the introduction of some principle equivalent in its effect to the institution of slavery,"[17] an argument carried to its fullest expression by George Fitzhugh's *Sociology for the South, or Free Society*

[12] Marius Robinson papers, Western Reserve Historical Society, Cleveland, and *Five Years' Progress of the Slave Power,* chapter 4. In addition, see *The Antislavery Bugle,* April 13, 1849, and *The National Era,* November 20, 1856, for remarks on the Cuban and Central American question; the same for December 8, 1849, and December 13, 1851, December 12, 1850, and February 19 and 26, 1851, on California; and for other charges, *The Antislavery Bugle,* May 26, 1855, and March 28, 1857, *The American Jubilee,* July and November, 1854, *The Radical Abolitionist,* II (August, 1856), p. 2–4, *Facts for the People,* December 1, 1855, and J. E. Cairnes, *op. cit.*, p. 60–64.

[13] "O. C. Freeman" (E. C. Rogers), *Letters on Slavery* (Boston, 1855), p. 63.

[14] See "How Can It Be Done?" *The Antislavery Record,* II (September, 1836); "To the Citizens of the United States," *The Philanthropist,* September 17, 1839; "To the Pennsylvania Hall Committee," *ibid.*, June 26, 1838; William Goodell, "Slavery Endangers Our Liberties," *The Antislavery Lecturer,* I (August, 1839); "The Slavepower Conspiracy against Civil Rights," *The Weekly Herald and Philanthropist,* June 25, 1845; and editorials in *The Radical Abolitionist,* December 26, 1837, *The National Antislavery Standard,* September 20, 1856, and *The Antislavery Bugle,* October 17, 1845.

[15] Explanations of the proslavery argument may be found in W. S. Jenkins, *Proslavery Thought in the Old South* (Chapel Hill, 1935), and A. Y. Lloyd, *The Slavery Controversy* (Chapel Hill, 1939).

[16] *The Philanthropist,* January 1, 1836; William Goodell, *Slavery and Antislavery* (Boston, 1852), p. 583; and James O'Neal, *The Workers in American History* (New York, 1921), p. 169.

[17] *The National Antislavery Standard,* November 8, 1856.

a Failure. Slavery was best for the laborer, providing for him a security and paternalistic benevolence lacking in a free competitive labor market; it was likewise best for the employer-capitalist, securing for him a contented, docile labor supply incapable of striking or demanding concessions. "By making the laborer himself capital," T. R. R. Cobb pointed out, "the conflict [of labor and capital] ceases"; adoption of the slavery principle in the Northern factory system would forever end the war between employer and laborer and result in greater advantages to both.[18] As slavery was superior to free society as an economic institution, so was it superior as a political system. Only upon slavery, said the South, could a truly stable republican government be built, for, as Hammond of South Carolina explained, it "prevented the ignorant, poor, and therefore untrustworthy and unstable portion of the population from exercising political influence."[19]

2

It was not difficult to perceive the implications of the pro-slavery argument. If slavery were a positive good, superior to free society as an economic, political, and social system, it was reasonable to assume that the next step of its proponents would be to impose it upon the nation at large.[20] Certain extreme statements from Southern fire-eaters invited some such interpretation. The Richmond *Enquirer,* for example, declared editorially that "the laws of the slave states justify the holding of white men in bondage," while the Richmond *Examiner* thought that "the principle of slavery is itself right, and does not depend upon difference in complexion," and that "slavery black or white is necessary." Similar quotations were endlessly reprinted by the abolitionist press, which agreed that extension of slavery to white men was a definite objective of the Slave Power.[21] And it could legally be done. The slave laws made no distinction in color; slavery was a matter of condition alone. If a person who was 99.9% white could, under the law, be claimed as a slave, the next step was a logical one. The only reason for the existence of pigmentation as a basis for slavery, warned the abolitionist, was simply that the Negro, who because of his helpless condition could be made a slave, happened to have a different color. The truth was that the institution did not rest upon a distinction of race at all; "where is the man," asked William Goodell, "who may not at any moment become a slave?" that is, if slavery is founded not upon color, but upon the right of the strong to enslave the weak?[22]

18 T. R. R. Cobb, *An Historical Sketch of Slavery . . .* (Philadelphia, 1858), p. ccxiv, and "A Citizen of Virginia," *The Union Past and Future* (4th ed., Charleston, 1850), p. 38. See also "The Blessings of Slavery," the Richmond *Examiner,* October 15 and 23, 1856; the Columbia, S. C., *Times,* and the Richmond *Examiner,* quoted by *The Antislavery Bugle,* January 20, 1855, September 20 and October 15, 1856; and R. K. Crallé, *The Works of John C. Calhoun* (New York, 1853–1855), III, p. 180.

19 *De Bow's Review,* VII (October, 1849), p. 296. For the development of the idea, see Calhoun Crallé, *op. cit.,* II, p. 362; Matthew Estes, *A Defense of Negro Slavery . . .* (Montgomery, Ala., 1846), p. 168–72; the Richmond *South,* July 8, 1858; "A Citizen of Virginia," *op. cit.,* p. 36–42; and the Richmond *Enquirer,* quoted by *The National Era,* August 9, 1855.

20 See J. G. Birney's analysis, *The Philanthropist,* July 29, 1836, and March 18, 1837.

21 Quotations from *The National Antislavery Standard,* October 11, 1856; G. M. Weston, *Who Are and Who May Be Slaves . . .* (n. p., 1856), p. 2; and *The Antislavery Bugle,* November 3, 1855. See also G. E. Baker, ed., *The Works of William N. Seward* (Boston, 1884–87), IV, p. 289–92, *The Radical Abolitionist,* October, 1857, and Garrison to the American Antislavery Association Anniversary, *The Antislavery Bugle,* June 2, 1855.

22 G. M. Weston, *op. cit.,* G. M. Stroud, *A Sketch*

In making their charges, the abolitionists made a particular effort to point out to the immigrant and the laborer, the two groups most likely to respond, the great stake they held in the abolition of slavery and the consequent defeat of the Slave Power. "American slavery," resolved the Massachusetts Antislavery Society in 1843, "is the deadliest foe of the rights of labor, and ought, therefore, to be the object of special indignation and alarm to the hardworking Irish immigrant." "What security have the Germans and Irish that their children will not, within a hundred years, be reduced to slavery in this the land of their adoption?" asked the Cincinnati *Freeman*. Involuntary servitude, it was warned, could legally be made a prerequisite to citizenship, and by some such device the Slave Power might introduce white slavery for the foreign-born.[23] As evidence, the abolitionists pointed to those provisions of the Nebraska bill which denied citizenship to territorial aliens for five years, and to the anti-foreign riots attendant to the Know-nothing movement. In general, the reaction of the foreign press, especially in the areas of German settlement, was sympathetic, while the influence of men such as C. C. Follen and Carl Schurz, both anti-slavery leaders, turned many immigrants toward the anti-slavery cause.[24] Yet in the end it was not the Slave Power threat which enlisted the support of the foreign-born in abolitionism, but other factors, primarily economic and political, and after 1856 and the decline of the nativistic troubles, the abolitionist campaign to convince the immigrant of the threat of white slavery was largely written off.

More successful was the appeal to the laboring classes. The workman, though little interested in the humanitarian aspects of the slavery question, intuitively perceived that his own liberties were to some extent involved in the issue. The existence of a slave labor system threatened his own status, and he could readily see that the competition of skilled and unskilled slaves tended to depreciate the value of free labor. "Wage slavery" and chattel slavery were, in the opinion of the wisest labor leaders, closely connected, and the former could not be successfully attacked until the latter were abolished.[25] For that matter, it was evident that wage slavery might conceivably turn into chattel slavery or something resembling it – the intervening step was a simple one – and the Slave Power threat held direct and personal meaning for the workman.

Nearly the whole structure of the proslavery argument could be turned to support the abolitionist contention that the Southern Slave Power intended to enslave white laborers. If slavery was the

of the Laws Relating to Slavery . . . (Philadelphia, 1856), chapter I; "An American," *America's Misfortune* (Buffalo, 1856); William Goodell, *The Antislavery Lecturer*, Nos. 8 and 9, I (August and September, 1839); and *The American Jubilee*, March, 1855. See Lincoln's lucid analysis of this problem, Nicolay and Hay, *Abraham Lincoln: A History* (New York, 1890), I, p. 178 f.

23 *The National Antislavery Standard*, January 4, 1844, *The Antislavery Bugle*, August 30, 1856, and *The American Jubilee*, January, 1855. Perhaps the clearest exposition of slavery's threat to the immigrant is Carl Schurz's Springfield speech of 1860, reprinted by *The National Era*, February 2, 1860.

24 German papers taking an anti-slavery stand included the New York *Staatszeitung* and *Abend Zeitung*, the Indiana *Freie Presse*, the Milwaukee *Volksfreund*, *Corsair*, and *Newsbode*, the Albany *Freie Blätter*, the Philadelphia *German National Gazette* and *Turnzeitung*, and the Cincinnati *Freeman*, *Hochwachter*, and *Turnzeitung*. The National Convention of Turners officially took an anti-slavery position in 1855; see *The National Era*, December 20, 1855, and January 17, 1856.

25 George E. McNeill, *The Labor Movement* (New York, 1887), p. 122.

best possible system for labor and capital, was it not logical to assume that it would be an improvement over free labor in the Northern factory system? If the laborer was unfitted for self-government, as the South argued, was it not implied that his employer should rule him? If slaves were much better off than the wage laborers, as Fitzhugh contended, the introduction of slavery into industry could be justified on the ground of bettering the free laborer's lot.[26] Such, said the abolitionist, was the intent of the Slave Power, and, if it gained political control of the federal government, it could realize its aim. It was not difficult to find and publicize extremely significant statements from the South. The Republican party in 1856 distributed a reprint of a South Carolina paper's belief that "Slavery is the natural state and normal condition of the laboring man, black or white." The Charleston *Mercury* thought that the great evil of free society was "a servile class of mechanics and laborers, unfit for self-government, and yet clothed with the attributes and powers of citizens." These, and similar statements from prominent Southerners, among them Leigh of Virginia, McDuffie of South Carolina, Calhoun, Dew, Fitzhugh, and others, made out a damaging case. "Let the whole country keep in mind," said Gamaliel Bailey, "that the Southern Democracy claims the right to enslave the whole laboring population of the country."[27] Neither were such sentiments restricted to the South. Solon Robinson of Indiana, a prominent agricultural authority, defended slavery as "a perfect labor system" and suggested its adoption on the nation's farms, a view that found some agreement in Ohio and Illinois.[28] The Salem *Register*, the Pittsburgh *Post*, the New York *Herald* and the extremely Southern New York *Day Book* thought slavery superior as a labor system, while in factory-conscious New England a debate was held on the question.[29] The abolitionist claim that the extension of slavery to white labor was something more than an impossible chimera had a point, and evidence to buttress it. If slavery were ever extended to include whites, the laborer, since his political and economic position was weakest, would be the first to be enslaved – a fact the abolitionists never allowed the laborer to forget. Thus, in 1839, *The Emancipator* summarized the issue: "The struggle is between the antagonist principles of free and slave labor. They cannot much longer co-exist. One must prevail to the exclusion of the other. The laborers will either be free, or enslaved."[30] Subsequent argument directed at Northern labor by the abolitionists deviated but little from this line, and they continued their appeal to the labor interests for assistance against the Slave Power until the Civil War.[31]

Although the laboring class was too disorganized and too politically immature during the period to exert much influence, nevertheless in the main the

[26] "What They Would Do If They Could," *The Philanthropist*, June 15, 1839, and *The Liberator*, March 12, 1836.

[27] James O'Neil, *op. cit.*, p. 169 f.; the New York *Daily Tribune*, November 9, 1854; G. M. Weston, *op. cit.*, p. 32; and *The National Era*, January 24, 1856.

[28] *De Bow's Review*, VII O. S. (September and November, 1849), 206–55, 379–89; *The National Antislavery Standard*, April 11, 1850; the Cincinnati *Weekly Herald and Philanthropist*, April 8, 1844; *The Antislavery Bugle*, October 21, 1854; and *Niles' Register*, XLVII, p. 57–60.

[29] *The Antislavery Bugle*, November 21, 1854, January 6 and 21, 1855, and December 6, 1856; and *The National Antislavery Standard*, February 1, 1850.

[30] Reprinted by *The Philanthropist*, June 15, 1839.

[31] Typical items include William Goodell, *A Full Statement . . .* (Boston, 1836), p. 22; *The Pro-*

effect of the abolitionist warnings of the Slave Power threat to its liberties was relatively large. In New England, especially, the workers tended to be anti-slavery partisans (the textile-mill girls were strongly abolitionist), but in other sections of the North some labor leaders felt that although the abolitionists were right in opposing slavery, they agitated the Negro question unduly. Other labor organizations, such as the Associationists, believed the real issue to be wage slavery, whose abolition must precede any other. "Down with all slavery, both chattel and wage," was a popular slogan in labor groups. Land Reformers, such as George Evans, thought that equal rights to the soil must precede abolition of slavery, else the root of the evil would never be eradicated.[32] But though laboring interests, divided as they were, could give the abolitionist movement little organized assistance, the long campaign to convince the laborer of the Slave Power threat brought individual support to the anti-slavery cause, and bore material fruit when, in the form of the Republican party, it entered its political phase.

ceedings of the Rhode Island Convention . . . (Providence, 1836), p. 39 f.; Birney and Gerrit Smith, *The Philanthropist*, February 19 and June 10, 1836; Garrison, *The Liberator*, December 1, 1837; Goodell, *The Antislavery Almanac*, 1838 ed., p. 6–8, and 1839 ed., p. 4 f., and *The Antislavery Lecturer*, no. 8 (August, 1839); "The Slaveholder and the Workman," *The Philanthropist*, November 4, 1840, and June 10, 1844; "The Labor Question," *The National Era*, July 31 and August 21, 1851; "Slavery . . . to Be Made the Universal Condition of the Laboring Classes," *The National Antislavery Standard*, October 11, 1856; and "Something for Laborers and Mechanics to Think About," *The Antislavery Bugle*, October 18, 1856.

[32] Herbert Harris, *American Labor* (New Haven, 1938), p. 59, and James Allen, *Reconstruction* (New York, 1937), p. 24 f. For treatments of the Associationist and Land Reform groups in abolition, see J. R. Commons, ed., *A Documentary History of American Industrial Society* (Cleveland, 1910). Especially interesting in this connection is *The Slavery of Poverty, with a Plan for Its Abolition* (New York, 1842), quarterly pamphlet number one of "The New York Society for the Abolition of ALL Slavery," a labor group.

3

The abolitionist contention, that there existed a Slave Power conspiracy which threatened the continuation of liberty, was an important factor in enlisting support among certain Northern elements for the anti-slavery movement. In some ways, and in some groups, the "great Slave Power plot" overshadowed in importance the religious, humanitarian, moral, and political issues of the controversy. The claim tended to discredit the pro-slavery argument, reading into it sinister implications; by carrying Southern logic to its ultimate conclusion and by identifying the slaveholder with a conspiracy of infinitely dangerous designs, the abolitionists robbed the pro-slavery position of any possible appeal to the immigrant, the workman, and the lower middle class in the North. Then too, the Slave Power threat helped widen the rift between North and South by making it more difficult than ever to be neutral toward or tolerant of slavery or its extension. Neutrality or tolerance, said the abolitionists, implied lack of interest in or positive hostility to the preservation of the liberal, democratic tradition. The issue simply admitted of no compromise. Identifying their cause with the greater cause of liberty, with republican government, and with the interests of large relatively unorganized special groups such as laborers or immigrants, the abolitionists made theirs the cause of civil and political freedom. The Slave Power threat personified the pro-slavery argument, made it vivid and concrete, and dramatized the controversy into a contest between good and evil, freedom and oppression, democracy and aristocracy. When war came, it was justified by the abolitionists and others as the last phase of the contest, as the final defense against the assaults of the Slave Power on traditional American rights. The South waged war, it was said, "... not against Abolitionism or Republicanism *per se,* but against free institutions and the democratic theory of government." Had it not been for the abolitionists, who awakened the people to the "villainous purposes and character of the Slave Power," we should have had "a nation in which were only two classes, *masters* and *slaves.*"[33]

Was there a Slave Power, and were the abolitionists correct in ascribing to it the evil designs which formed so large and important a part of the abolitionist propaganda? In the sense of the term as used by Wilson, Goodell, Bailey, Garrison, and others – a secret and highly organized group with conscious aims of imposing restrictions upon traditional liberties – the Slave Power conspiracy probably had no real existence. The South was never so completely unified as to warrant evidence of a definite "conspiracy." There was Southern disagreement upon such vital issues as Texas annexation, the Mexican War, the Wilmot Proviso, the 1850 Compromise, and the Kansas question.[34] However, it is clear that among Southern leaders there was unity of belief that slavery was a good system, probably the best, and that it should be retained and extended; the events of the period from 1830 to 1860 showed that in preserving and extending it the South was willing to infringe upon basic civil and personal rights, free speech, free press, free thought, and constitutional liberty.[35] The Calhoun-Fitzhugh school of thought, that slavery was a "positive good," was more than a defense of slavery; it was a counterattack upon free society, one which commanded excellent support in the South and, the abolitionist believed, significant support in the North. While the "conspiracy" of which the abolitionists warned was no doubt a natural alliance of common political and economic interests, its threat to liberty, North and South, was more than idle. There were too many public utterances of policy (emanating often, it is true, from extremists, but at the same time from Southern leaders) for the times to disregard William Goodell's warning that "*the South is thoroughly in earnest.* She is no land of *shams.* There is reality, terrible reality there."[36] The alliance itself was motivated by and founded upon the cardinal principle of slavery – the master principle[37] – and the abolitionists were not so far wrong in believing that its existence seriously jeopardized, for the first time since the founding of the republic, the American tradition.

[33] Anonymous, *Southern Hatred of Free Institutions* (Boston, 1862), p. 10, and Marius Robinson, undated lecture notes, Western Reserve Historical Society. Abolitionists consistently claimed credit for arousing the North to a defense of freedom, and for unifying it in the final struggle; see H. W. Beecher, in *Patriotic Addresses* (Boston, 1887), and Wendell Phillips, *Speeches, Lectures, and Letters* (Boston, 1870, p. 52).

[34] See C. S. Boucher, "*In re* That Aggressive Slaveocracy," *Mississippi Valley Historical Review* (June–September, 1921), p. 13–80.

[35] See R. B. Nye, "Civil Liberties and the Antislavery Controversy," *Science and Society,* IX (Spring, 1945), p. 125–147.

[36] *The American Jubilee,* June, 1854.

[37] See the admirable analysis of the political thought of John C. Calhoun, one of the most influential of Southern leaders, by Richard N. Current, "John C. Calhoun, Philosopher of Reaction," *The Antioch Review* (Summer, 1943), p. 223–34.

Charles and Mary Beard: THE APPROACH OF THE IRREPRESSIBLE CONFLICT

HAD the economic systems of the North and the South remained static or changed slowly without effecting immense dislocations in the social structure, the balance of power might have been maintained indefinitely by repeating the compensatory tactics of 1787, 1820, 1833, and 1850; keeping in this manner the inherent antagonisms within the bounds of diplomacy. But nothing was stable in the economy of the United States or in the moral sentiments associated with its diversities.

Within each section of the country, the necessities of the productive system were generating portentous results. The periphery of the industrial vortex of the Northeast was daily enlarging, agriculture in the Northwest was being steadily supplemented by manufacturing, and the area of virgin soil open to exploitation by planters was diminishing with rhythmic regularity – shifting with mechanical precision the weights which statesmen had to adjust in their efforts to maintain the equilibrium of peace. Within each of the three sections also occurred an increasing intensity of social concentration as railways, the telegraph, and the press made travel and communication cheap and almost instantaneous, facilitating the centripetal process that was drawing people of similar economic status and parallel opinions into cooperative activities. Finally the intellectual energies released by accumulating wealth and growing leisure – stimulated by the expansion of the reading public and the literary market – developed with deepened accuracy the word-patterns of the current social persuasions, contributing with galvanic effect to the consolidation of identical groupings.

As the years passed, the planting leaders of Jefferson's agricultural party insisted with mounting fervor that the opposition, first of the Whigs and then of the Republicans, was at bottom an association of interests formed for the purpose of plundering productive management and labor on the land. And with steadfast insistence they declared that in the insatiable greed of their political foes lay the source of the dissensions which were tearing the country asunder.

"There is not a pursuit in which man is engaged (agriculture excepted)," exclaimed Reuben Davis of Mississippi in 1860, "which is not demanding legislative aid to enable it to enlarge its profits and all at the expense of the primary pursuit of man – agriculture. . . . Those interests, having a common purpose of plunder, have united and combined to use the government as the instrument of their operation and have thus virtually converted it into a consolidated empire. Now this combined host of interests stands arrayed against the agricultural states; and this is the reason of the conflict which like an earthquake is shaking our political fabric to its foundation." The furor over slavery is a mere subterfuge to cover other purposes. "Relentless avarice stands firm with its iron heel upon the Constitution." This creature, "incorporated avarice," has chained "the agricultural states to the northern rock" and lives like a vulture upon their prosperity. It is the effort of Prometheus to burst his manacles that provokes the assault on slavery. "These states struggle like a giant," continued Davis, "and alarm these incorporated interests, lest they may break the chain that binds them to usurpation; and therefore they are making this fierce onslaught upon the slave property of the southern states."

The fact that free-soil advocates waged war only on slavery in the territories was to Jefferson Davis conclusive proof of an underlying conspiracy against agriculture. He professed more respect for the abolitionist than for the freesoiler. The former, he said, is dominated by an honest conviction that slavery is wrong everywhere and that all men ought to be free; the latter does not assail slavery in the states – he merely wishes to abolish it in the territories that are in due course to be admitted to the Union.

With challenging directness, Davis turned upon his opponents in the Senate and charged them with using slavery as a blind to delude the unwary: "What do you propose, gentlemen of the Free-Soil party? Do you propose to better the condition of the slave? Not at all. What then do you propose? You say you are opposed to the expansion of slavery. . . . Is the slave to be benefited by it? Not at all. It is not humanity that influences you in the position which you now occupy before the country. . . . It is that you may have an opportunity of cheating us that you want to limit slave territory within circumscribed bounds. It is that you may have a majority in the Congress of the United States and convert the Government into an engine of northern aggrandizement. It is that your section may grow in power and prosperity upon treasures unjustly taken from the South, like the vampire bloated and gorged with the blood which it has secretly sucked from its victim. . . . You desire to weaken the political power of the southern states; and why? Because you want, by an unjust system of legislation, to promote the industry of the New England states, at the expense of the people of the South and their industry."

Such in the mind of Jefferson Davis, fated to be president of the Confederacy, was the real purpose of the party which sought to prohibit slavery in the territories; that party did not declare slavery to be a moral disease calling for the severe remedy of the surgeon; it merely sought to keep bondage out of the new states as they came into the Union – with one fundamental aim in view, namely, to gain political ascendancy in the government of the United States and fasten upon the country an economic policy that meant the exploitation of the South for the benefit of northern capitalism.

But the planters were after all fighting against the census returns, as the phrase of the day ran current. The amazing growth of northern industries, the rapid extension of railways, the swift expansion of foreign trade to the ends of the earth, the attachment of the farming regions of the West to the centers of manufacture and finance through transportation and credit, the destruction of state consciousness by migration, the alien invasion, the erection of new commonwealths in the Valley of Democracy, the nationalistic drive of interstate commerce, the increase of population in the North, and the southward pressure of the capitalistic glacier all conspired to assure the ultimate triumph of what the orators were fond of calling "the free labor system." This was a dynamic thrust far too powerful for planters operating in a limited territory with incompetent labor on soil of diminishing fertility. Those who swept forward with it, exulting in the approaching triumph of machine industry, warned the planters of their ultimate subjection.

To statesmen of the invincible forces recorded in the census returns, the planting opposition was a huge, compact, and self-conscious economic association bent upon political objects — the possession of the government of the United States, the protection of its interests against adverse legislation, dominion over the territories, and enforcement of the national fugitive slave law throughout the length and breadth of the land. No phrase was more often on the lips of northern statesmen than "the slave power." The pages of the Congressional Globe bristled with references to "the slave system" and its influence over the government of the country. But it was left for William H. Seward of New York to describe it with a fullness of familiar knowledge that made his characterization a classic.

Seward knew from experience that a political party was no mere platonic society engaged in discussing abstractions. "A party," he said, "is in one sense a joint stock association, in which those who contribute most direct the action and management of the concern. The slaveholders contributing in an overwhelming proportion to the capital strength of the Democratic party, they necessarily dictate and prescribe its policy. The inevitable caucus system enables them to do this with a show of fairness and justice." This class of slaveholders, consisting of only three hundred and forty-seven thousand persons, Seward went on to say, was spread from the banks of the Delaware to the banks of the Rio Grande; it possessed nearly all the real estate in that section, owned more than three million other "persons" who were denied all civil and political rights, and inhibited "freedom of speech, freedom of press, freedom of the ballot box, freedom of education, freedom of literature, and freedom of popular assemblies. . . . The slaveholding class has become the governing power in each of the slaveholding states and it practically chooses thirty of the sixty-two members of the Senate, ninety of the two hundred and thirty-three members of the House of Representatives, and one hundred and five of the two hundred and ninety-five electors of the President and Vice-President of the United States."

Becoming still more concrete, Seward accused the President of being "a confessed apologist of the slave-property class." Examining the composition of the Senate, he found the slave-owning group in possession of all the important committees. Peering into the House of Representatives he discovered no impregnable bulwark of freedom there. Nor did respect for judicial ermine compel him to spare the Supreme Court. With irony he exclaimed: "How fitting does the proclamation of its opening close with the invocation: 'God save the United States and this honorable court'. . . . The court consists of a chief justice and eight associate justices. Of these five were called from slave states and four from free states. The opinions and bias of each of them were carefully considered by the President and Senate when he was appointed. Not one of them was found wanting in soundness of politics, according to the slaveholder's exposition of the Constitution, and those who were called from the free states were even more distinguished in that respect than their brethren from the slaveholding states."

Seward then analyzed the civil service of the national government and could descry not a single person among the thousands employed in the post office, the treasury, and other great departments who was "false to the slaveholding interest." Under the spoils system, the dominion of the slavocracy extended into all branches of the federal administration. "The customs-houses and the public lands pour forth two golden streams – one into the elections to procure votes for the slaveholding class; and the other into the treasury to be enjoyed by those whom it shall see fit to reward with places in the public service." Even in the North, religion, learning, and the press were under the spell of this masterful class, frightened lest they incur its wrath.

Having described the gigantic operating structure of the slavocracy, Seward drew with equal power a picture of the opposing system founded on "free labor." He surveyed the course of economy in the North – the growth of industry, the spread of railways, the swelling tide of European immigration, and the westward roll of free farmers – rounding out the country, knitting it together, bringing "these antagonistic systems" continually into closer contact. Then he uttered those fateful words which startled conservative citizens from Maine to California – words of prophecy which proved to be brutally true – "the irrepressible conflict."

This inexorable clash, he said, was not "accidental, unnecessary, the work of interested or fanatical agitators and therefore ephemeral." No. "It is an irrepressible conflict between opposing and enduring forces." The hopes of those who sought peace by appealing to slave owners to reform themselves were as chaff in a storm. "How long and with what success have you waited already for that reformation? Did any property class ever so reform itself? Did the patricians in old Rome, the noblesse or clergy in France? The landholders in Ireland? The landed aristocracy in England? Does the slaveholding class even seek to beguile you with such a hope? Has it not become rapacious, arrogant, defiant?" All attempts at compromise were "vain and ephemeral." There was accordingly but one supreme task before the people of the United States – the task of confounding and overthrowing "by one decisive blow the betrayers of the Constitution and freedom forever." In uttering this indictment, this prophecy soon to be fulfilled with such appalling accuracy, Seward stepped beyond the bounds of cautious politics and read himself out of the little group of men who were eligible for the Republican nomination in 1860. Frantic efforts to soften his words by explanations and additions could not appease his critics.

Given an irrepressible conflict which could be symbolized in such unmistakable patterns by competent interpreters of opposing factions, a transfer of the issues from the forum to the field, from the conciliation of diplomacy to the decision of arms was bound to come. Each side obdurately bent upon its designs and convinced of its rectitude, by the fulfillment of its wishes precipitated events and effected distributions of power that culminated finally in the tragedy foretold by Seward. Those Democrats who operated on historic knowledge rather than on prophetic insight, recalling how many times the party of Hamilton had been crushed at elections, remembering how the Whigs had never been able to carry the country on a cleancut Webster-Clay program, and counting upon the continued support of a huge array of farmers and mechanics marshaled behind the planters, imagined apparently that politics — viewed as the science of ballot enumeration — could resolve the problems of power raised by the maintenance of the Union.

And in this opinion they were confirmed by the outcome of the presidential campaign in 1852, when the Whigs, with General Winfield Scott, a hero of the Mexican war, at their head, were thoroughly routed by the Democratic candidate, General Franklin Pierce of New Hampshire. Indeed the verdict of the people was almost savage, for Pierce carried every state but four, receiving 254 out of 296 electoral votes. The Free-Soil party that branded slavery as a crime and called for its prohibition in the territories scarcely made a ripple, polling only 156,000 out of more than three million votes, a figure below the record set in the previous campaign.

With the Whigs beaten and the Free-Soilers evidently a dwindling handful of negligible critics, exultant Democrats took possession of the Executive offices and Congress, inspired by a firm belief that their tenure was secure. Having won an overwhelming victory on a definite tariff for revenue and pro-slavery program, they acted as if the party of Hamilton was for all practical purposes as powerless as the little band of abolitionist agitators. At the succeeding election in 1856 they again swept the country — this time with James Buchanan of Pennsylvania as their candidate. Though his triumph was not as magisterial as that of Pierce it was great enough to warrant a conviction that the supremacy of the Democratic party could not be broken at the polls.

During these eight years of tenure, a series of events occurred under Democratic auspices, which clinched the grasp of the planting interest upon the country and produced a correlative consolidation of the opposition. One line of development indicated an indefinite extension of the slave area; another the positive withdrawal of all government support from industrial and commercial enterprise. The first evidence of the new course came in the year immediately following the inauguration of Pierce. In 1854, Congress defiantly repealed the Missouri Compromise and threw open to slavery the vast section of the Louisiana Purchase which had been closed to it by the covenant adopted more than three decades before. On the instant came a rush of slavery champions from Missouri into Kansas determined to bring it into the southern sphere of influence. Not content with the conquest of the forbidden West, filibustering parties under pro-slavery leaders attempted to seize Cuba and Nicaragua and three American ministers abroad flung out to the world a flaming proclamation, known as the "Ostend Manifesto," which declared that the United States would be justified in wresting Cuba from Spain by force — acts of imperial aggression which even the Democratic administration in Washington felt constrained to repudiate.

Crowning the repeal of the Missouri Compromise came two decisions of the Supreme Court giving sanction to the expansion of slavery in America and assuring high protection for that peculiar institution even in the North. In the Dred Scott case decided in March, 1857, Chief Justice Taney declared in effect that the Missouri Compromise had been void from the beginning and that Congress had no power under the Constitution to prohibit slavery in the territories of the United States anywhere at any time. This legal triumph for the planting interest was followed in 1859 by another decision in which the Supreme Court upheld the fugitive slave law and all the drastic procedure provided for its enforcement. To the frightened abolitionists it seemed that only one more step was needed to make freedom unconstitutional throughout the country.

These extraordinary measures on behalf of slavery were accompanied by others that touched far more vitally economic interests in the North. In 1859, the last of the subsidies for trans-Atlantic steamship companies was ordered discontinued by Congress. In 1857, the tariff was again reduced, betraying an unmistakable drift of the nation toward free trade. In support of this action, the representatives of the South and Southwest were almost unanimous and they gathered into their fold a large number of New England congressmen on condition that no material reductions should be made in duties on cotton goods. On the other hand, the Middle States and the West offered a large majority against tariff reduction so that the division was symptomatic.

Immediately after the new revenue law went into effect an industrial panic burst upon the country, spreading distress among business men and free laborers. While that tempest was running high, the paper money anarchy let loose by the Democrats reached the acme of virulence as the notes of wildcat banks flooded the West and South and financial institutions crashed in every direction, fifty-one failing in Indiana alone within a period of five years. Since all hope of reviving Hamilton's system of finance had been buried, those who believed that a sound currency was essential to national prosperity were driven to the verge of desperation. On top of these economic calamities came Buchanan's veto of the Homestead bill which the impatient agrarians had succeeded in getting through Congress in a compromise form – an act of presidential independence which angered the farmers and mechanics who regarded the national domain as their own inheritance.

Two incidents in this series of startling events deserve special consideration on account of their prominence in the forensics that decorated the struggle; namely, the repeal of the Missouri Compromise and the Dred Scott decision. In connection with the organization of two new western territories, Kansas and Nebraska, in 1854, Congress provided that, when they were admitted to the Union, they could come in, with or without slavery, as their respective constitutions might provide. Since these territories lay north of the Missouri Compromise line, the provision in effect set aside the solemn understanding which had bound the two sections of the country for so many years. To clear up all doubts, Congress expressly declared that the Missouri covenant of 1820 was null and void as contrary to the principle of non-intervention with the institution of slavery in the territories.

The authorship of this program is generally ascribed to Stephen A. Douglas, a Democratic Senator from Illinois, and his action in the premises imputed to his overweening desire to become President of the United States. Though Douglas took upon himself both the onus and the honor of the repeal, Senator Atchison of Missouri, a spokesman of local slave owners eager to break over into the rich region to the west, claimed to have inspired the stroke. The nature of American politics lends plausibility to this latter view.

However, the point is not important. The significant feature of the maneuver was the vote on the repeal in Congress. In the Senate fourteen southern Democrats, nine southern Whigs, and fourteen northern Democrats voted in favor of the bill; while four northern Democrats, six northern Whigs, two free-Soilers, one southern Democrat, and one southern Whig voted against it. In short, two southern votes were recorded against the measure in the Upper Chamber. Of the hundred votes cast against it in the House of Representatives, only nine came from the slave states while forty-two Democrats from the North broke from their party and joined the dissenters. Considered in any light, the division was ominous: the repeal represented the demand of an almost solid South supported by a wing of the northern Democrats – effecting a triumph for the planters that fell only a little bit below Calhoun's extreme demand. True, the Kansas-Nebraska act did not absolutely force slavery upon the states to be admitted from the region in question but it made slavery lawful in the territories and permitted the residents to decide the ultimate question for themselves.

Just one more legal step was essential to win for the planting interest the whole territorial domain of the nation, and secure its weight in the balance of power apparently for all time. That step was a decision by the Supreme Court declaring that Congress had no authority under the Constitution to abolish or prohibit slavery in any of the territories. If the Constitution could be so interpreted, then either a reversal of the decision or an amendment would be necessary before Congress could undo the effect of the decree. Since the judges held for life and the approval of the Senate was necessary to new appointments, the possibility of getting a fresh reading of the auspices was remote. On the other hand, approval by three-fourths of the states being required for the adoption of an amendment, a reversal by that means was inconceivable. If the coveted interpretation could be obtained, the planting states would be safe forever. At least so it seemed to those wise in their generation. But one point was overlooked in the calculations, namely, the likelihood of revolution.

Either by accident or intent the great issue was presented to the Supreme Court in 1856 by the celebrated Dred Scott case. Scott was a slave who had been taken by his master into the upper Louisiana territory in the days when, theoretically at least, the Missouri Compromise was still in force and slavery was forbidden in that region. After a term of residence there, the bondman had been returned to the state of Missouri where he sued for his liberty on the ground of having been in free territory. Was he then a free man or a slave? The whole affair could have been put under that simple rubric.

The Supreme Court could have answered the question in a few words without mentioning the Missouri Compromise or the power of Congress to abolish slavery in the territories owned by the United States. With perfect ease, the judges could have disposed of the case by saying: "Whatever was the status of Scott in the upper Louisiana region while he was there, he was restored to bondage on his return to slave soil and is now a slave." Indeed when the matter was first argued, a majority of the Court agreed among themselves that the issue should be decided without discussing the thorny question that was agitating the country. But after reaching this agreement, the majority for various reasons changed their minds and in the end Chief Justice Taney rendered an opinion not vital to the disposition of the case in which he declared that the act of Congress, known as the Missouri Compromise, was null and void; that Congress could not constitutionally abolish slavery in the territories. Thus he gave a stunning blow to the young Republican party whose cardinal doctrine was that Congress should establish freedom in all the territories; and evidently he had ignored all anti-slavery agitators of every sort and condition.

Thinking that the issue had now been settled by a decree of final authority, statesmen from the South called upon their countrymen to show proper respect for the highest tribunal in the land, a counsel of loyalty natural enough in the circumstances. And yet in a reaction equally natural, the Republicans rejected the advice. Under their influence northern legislatures denounced the opinion of Chief Justice Taney as extra-judicial in character, as sheer usurpation, and without binding effect upon the people. In Congress and outside, Democrats were taunted with having once opposed the constitutionality of the United States Bank after Chief Justice Marshall had set his high seal of legal approval upon it. Into their teeth Republican leaders flung quotations from Jefferson's attacks upon the Supreme Court made long before on similar occasions when that tribunal had pretended to act as the final arbiter in constitutional conflicts.

Convinced that the decision was a political trick, Abraham Lincoln said that, while Republicans would accept the decree of the Court remanding Scott to servitude, they would frankly reject its opinion respecting the power of Congress over slavery itself. Elaborating this idea, he declared that the President and Congress ought to disregard Taney's opinion as a rule of law, that slavery ought to be abolished in the territories in spite of the doctrines announced by the Court, and that the opinion ought to be reversed by a peaceful method — meaning of course a reconstruction of the Court through an efficient use of the appointing power. It had been done by Jacksonian Democracy. It could be done again.

The more Lincoln thought about the Dred Scott case, the hotter became his resentment. Finally he broke out in a militant note: "Familiarize yourselves with the chains of bondage and you prepare your own limbs to wear them. Accustomed to trample on the rights of others, you have lost the genius of your own independence and become the fit subjects of the first cunning tyrant who rises among you. And let me tell you, that all these things are prepared for you by the teachings of history, if the elections shall promise that the next Dred Scott decision and all future decisions will be quietly acquiesced in by the people."

Going beyond this view, some of his party colleagues openly denounced the action of the Court as a political conspiracy arranged by the President, certain members of Congress, and the pro-slavery judges of the Court for the purpose of fastening chattel bondage upon the territories forever. This extreme contention they rested on mere incidents. It so happened that Buchanan, in his inaugural address on March 4, 1857, a few days before the opinion of the Court in the Dred Scott case was made public, referred to the forthcoming decision and expressed his intention, in common with all other good citizens, to submit cheerfully to the ruling of the Court, "whatever this may be." To Senator Seward, Republican leader from New York, the President's declaration was sheer mockery. In a terrific indictment delivered in the Senate, he asserted that Buchanan "approached or was approached by the Supreme Court of the United States," arranged with that tribunal to hang the millstone of slavery on the neck of the people of Kansas, and knew very well when he blandly promised to abide by the will of the Court just what its decision would be.

Naturally this charge made a tremendous sensation, bringing down on the Senator's head the severest criticism from conservatives. On all sides he was accused of making assertions for which he had not the slightest proof. Indeed his attack was seemingly so rash and so unjustified that for more than half a century even northern historians agreed in condemning it. Professor John W. Burgess, for example, after looking over the evidence available in 1899, when he wrote on the middle period, declared that "both Mr. Buchanan and Mr. Taney were men of the highest personal and official character and possessed the most delicate sense of the requirements and proprieties of the great stations which they occupied. It is almost certain that the charge was an unfounded suspicion." James Ford Rhodes, in the first edition of his history, later modified, was still more emphatic: collusion between Buchanan and the impeccable Taney was simply impossible.

There the matter rested until the publication of President Buchanan's papers in 1910 revealed a portion of the truth. Among those records was a note from Justice Catron of the Supreme Court, dated February 19, 1857, thirteen days before the inaugural address in question – a note in which the Justice informs Buchanan that the constitutionality of the Missouri Compromise line will be decided by the Court shortly in the Dred Scott case and asks the President-elect to write to Justice Grier stating how necessary it is to "settle the agitation by an affirmative decision of the Supreme Court, the one way or the other." Acting on the suggestion Buchanan wrote to Justice Grier; just what we do not know for it seems the letter has been lost. Apparently he urged the Justice to fall in line; at all events a reply from Grier, dated February 23, 1857 – nine days before the inauguration – acknowledges the receipt of a communication from Buchanan, gives a brief history of the Dred Scott case, discusses the forthcoming decision of the Court, states that the Missouri Compromise line will be declared invalid, and adds that the opinion will be rendered by March 6th. The Justice then concludes: "Though contrary to our usual practice, we have thought it due to you to state in candor and confidence the real state of the matter." So Senator Seward had a stronger foundation for his indictment than he himself imagined.

For a brief moment after the publication of the Buchanan papers, it looked as if the Dred Scott decision had really been framed by the President of the United States and certain Justices of the Supreme Court, but later revelations gave the matter still another aspect. Within a few years certain records belonging to Justice McLean of the Supreme Court were placed in the Library of Congress, opening to students a new chapter in the story of this crucial case.

In the light of unquestionable evidence, it appears that, when the majority of the judges decided at first to avoid the vexatious issue of the Missouri Compromise, Justice McLean announced to them his intention to file a dissenting opinion in the nature of a stump speech maintaining the power of Congress to abolish slavery in the territories — sound doctrine according to the politics of the Republican party. Now Justice McLean, like so many others in his day, was consumed by the ambition to be President of the United States and was in fact a strenuous seeker for that high office during more than a decade. Beyond question, he attempted to wring the nomination from the Republicans in 1856 and he sent active agents to present his appeal in Chicago four years later. And the dissenting opinion which he finally filed in the Dred Scott case upheld the power of Congress to exclude slavery from the territories, thus in effect setting forth the very political principles which he authorized his workers to employ in the quest for the Republican prize.

Beyond doubt accordingly the stiff insistence of Justice McLean upon the promulgation of his views at all costs was a leading factor in forcing the pro-slavery judges to come out against the validity of the Missouri Compromise. They were also aided in arriving at this conclusion by the knowledge that Wayne, a southern Justice, would announce pro-slavery doctrines in a dissenting opinion if they did not squarely face the issue. So the ambitions and passions of both political parties were in reality responsible for the judicial opinion that rocked the country from one end to the other. At any rate the Dred Scott decision was not a deliberate conspiracy on the part of the slavocracy.

The amazing acts of mastery — legislative, executive, judicial — committed by the federal government in the decade between 1850 and 1860 changed the whole political climate of America. They betrayed a growing consolidation in the planting group, its increased dominance in the Democratic party, and an evident determination to realize its economic interests and protect its labor system at all hazards. In a kind of doom, they seemed to mark the final supremacy of the political army which had swept into office with Andrew Jackson. During the thirty-two years between that event and the inauguration of Lincoln, the Democrats controlled the Presidency and the Senate for twenty-four years, the Supreme Court for twenty-six years, and the House of Representatives for twenty-two years. By the end of the period, the old farmer-labor party organized by Jackson had passed under the dominion of the planting interest and the farming wing of the North was confronted with the alternative of surrender or secession.

In this shift of power the Whigs of the South, discovering the tendencies of the popular balloting, moved steadily over into the Democratic camp. Though unavoidable, the transfer was painful; the planting Whigs, being rich and influential, had little affection for the white farmers who rallied around the Jacksonian banner. According to the estimate of a southern newspaper in 1850, the Whigs owned at least three-fourths of all the slaves in the country and it was a matter of common knowledge that leaders among them disliked wildcat banking as much as they hated high duties on the manufactured goods they bought. Indeed to a southern gentleman of the old school the radical agrarianism of Andrew Johnson was probably more odious than the tariff schedules devised by Daniel Webster. It was said that one of them, when asked whether a gentleman could be a Democrat, snapped back the tart reply: "Well, he is not apt to be; but if he is, he is in damned bad company."

But the rich planters were relatively few in numbers and virtue was subject to the law of necessity; the populace had the votes, northern manufacturers were demanding protection, abolitionists were agitating, and in the end all but the most conservative remnant of the southern Whigs had to go over to the party that professed the dangerous doctrines of Jackson. The achievements of the years that lay between 1850 and 1860 seemed to justify the sacrifice.

Though the drift toward the irrepressible conflict was steady and strong, as events revealed, the politics of the decade had the outward semblances of dissolution. The abolitionists and free-soilers, while a mere minority as we have seen, were able to worry the politicians of both parties in the North. Largely deserted by their southern cohorts, the Whigs, whose organization had always been tenuous at best, could discover no way of mustering a majority of votes on the bare economic policies of Hamilton and Webster. Their two victories – in 1840 and 1848 – had been dubious and their only hope for a triumph at the polls lay in a combination with other factors.

To this confusion in party affairs, the intellectual and religious ferment of the age added troublesome factional disputes. A temperance element, strong enough to carry prohibition in a few states, was giving the politicians anxiety in national campaigns. A still more formidable cabal, the Know Nothing, or American Party, sprang up in the current opposition to foreigners, the papacy, infidelity, and socialism. Combining the functions of a party and a fraternal order, it nominated candidates for office and adopted secret rites, dark mysteries, grips, and passwords which gave it an atmosphere of uncertain vitality. Members were admitted by solemn ceremony into full fellowship with "The Supreme Order of the Star-spangled Banner," whose "daily horror and nightly specter was the pope." When asked about their principles, they replied mysteriously: "I know nothing." Appealing to deep-seated emotions, this movement showed strength in many localities and was only dissolved by the smashing energy of more momentous issues.

The signal for a general realignment of factions and parties was given by the passage of the Kansas-Nebraska bill of 1854 repealing the Missouri Compromise. In fact, while that measure was pending in Congress a coalescing movement was to be observed: northern Whigs persuaded that their old party was moribund, Democrats weary of planting dominance, and free-soilers eager to exclude slavery from the territories began to draw together to resist the advance of the planting power. In February of that year, a number of Whigs and Democrats assembled at Ripon, Wisconsin, and resolved that a new party must be formed if the bill passed.

When the expected event occurred, the Ripon insurgents created a fusion committee and chose the name "Republican" as the title of their young political association. In July, a Michigan convention composed of kindred elements demanded the repeal of the Kansas-Nebraska act, the repeal of the fugitive slave law, and the abolition of slavery in the District of Columbia. This convention also agreed to postpone all differences "with regard to political economy or administrative policy" and stay in the field as a "Republican" party until the struggle against slavery extension was finished. All over the country similar meetings were mustered and the local cells of the new national party rose into being. Meanwhile the old Whigs who wanted peace and prosperity were floating about looking for any drifting wreckage that might hold them above the waves.

As the election of 1856 approached, the Republicans made ready to enter the national field. After a preliminary conference at Pittsburgh, they held a national convention at Philadelphia and nominated for the presidency John C. Frémont, the Western explorer, a son-in-law of Benton, the faithful Jacksonian Democrat. In their platform they made the exclusion of slavery from the territories – and of necessity its economic and political implications – the paramount issue. So restricted, the platform offered no prizes to regular Whigs, no tariff, banking, or currency reforms; rather did it appeal to the farmers of the Jeffersonian school – men who were not slave owners and did not expect to enter that class, men who were determined to keep slavery out of the territories and to make the federal domain an estate for free farmers.

Lest there be some misunderstanding, they made it clear throughout their campaign that they were not trying to revive the Federalist or the Whig party. They were conscious of the fact that the name "Republican" of which they boasted was the device chosen by Jefferson for his embattled farmers and used by his followers until they fell under the sway of Jackson. "There is not a plank in our platform," exclaimed one of the Republican orators from Wisconsin before the great accommodation of 1860, "which does not conform to the principles of Jefferson; the man who, of all others, has ever been regarded as the true representative of the Republican party of this country. He was its representative in the Congress of 1776. He was its leader and representative in 1800; he was its true representative in 1812; he is the true representative of the Republican party to-day. We stand, Sir, upon his doctrines and we fight for his principles. We stand upon no sectional platform; we present no sectional issues . . . and we are coming to take possession of this government, to administer it for the whole country, North and South; and suffer monopolists neither of the North or the South to control its administration and so shape its action as to subserve the interests of the aristocratic few." On this platform those who opposed the plutocracy of the East and the planting aristocracy of the South could easily unite.

Replying to the Republican challenge the Democratic organization granted to its pro-slavery wing almost every demand. In its platform of 1856 it reiterated as a matter of course its fixed agricultural creed: no protective tariffs, no national banks, no industrial subsidies, and no Hamiltonian devices. It then commended the bargain of 1850, endorsed slavery as an institution, approved the repeal of the Missouri Compromise, and proposed that the new states to be admitted to the Union should come in with or without slavery as their constitutions might provide. In exchange the northern wing received honorific compensation in the nomination of James Buchanan of Pennsylvania. The South thus got the platform; the North, the candidate.

Defied by the Democrats in front and menaced by the Republicans on the left, the old Whigs, who hated the bother of slavery agitation and merely wanted to get government support for business enterprise, were sorely perplexed. They saw their southern brethren drawn away by the Democratic gift of the Kansas-Nebraska bill and yet they could not find in the Republican platform a promise of protection for industry or a pledge of currency reform. On the face of things, a combination with either of these political associations was impossible and so the Whigs decided to tempt the fates again and alone. At a convention held in Baltimore, they condemned "geographical parties," expressed a reverence for the Constitution and the Union, and nominated Millard Fillmore, a man "eminent for his calm and pacific temperament." As Fillmore had already been blessed by the American, or Know Nothing, party, there was some prospect of effecting a formidable bloc under his leadership.

When the votes were counted in the autumn of 1856, it was clear that a great majority of the people were opposed to anti-slavery agitation in every form. Not only was Buchanan elected by a safe margin on a strong slavery program; he and Fillmore together polled nearly three million votes against less than half that figure cast for Frémont. In other words, Garrison had been at work for a quarter of a century when, by a decision of more than two to one, even the mildest plank in the anti-slavery platform was overwhelmingly repudiated by the country at large. Still Frémont's poll revealed an immense gain in the number of free-soilers as compared with their trivial strength at previous contests, demonstrating in a striking manner that the fight for the possession of the territories, with all it implied in terms of political and economic power at Washington, could not be avoided. Especially did it show the Whigs that they would have to work out a new combination of forces if they expected to get business enterprise on an even keel again.

Fortunately for them, the way to the solution of their problem was pointed out by the election returns: Fillmore had received 874,000 votes, a number which, added to Frémont's total, would have elected a candidate. Given these figures, the question of how to unite free-soil farmers and timid apostles of prosperity became therefore the supreme issue before the political leaders who took their bearings after the storm of 1856 in the hope of finding some method of ousting the Democrats at the next tourney. Neither group could win without the other; the union of either with the planting aristocracy was impossible. Obviously an accommodation – a readjustment of the balance of power – and the right kind of candidate offered to Whigs and free-soil Republicans the only assurance of ultimate victory.

"The Government has fallen into the hands of the Slave Power completely," wrote Wendell Phillips in 1854. "So far as national politics are concerned, we are beaten – there's no hope. We shall have Cuba in a year or two, Mexico in five, and I should not wonder if efforts were made to revive the slave trade, though perhaps unsuccessfully, as the northern slave states, which live by the export of slaves, would help us in opposing that. Events hurry forward with amazing rapidity; we live fast here. The future seems to unfold a vast slave empire united with Brazil and darkening the whole West. I hope I may be a false prophet, but the sky was never so dark."

Three years later, when the inauguration of Buchanan had turned discouragement into despair, the only strategic stroke that Phillips and his colleagues could invent was to hold an abolition convention in Massachusetts and adopt a solemn slogan calling for the disruption of the Union with the slave states. And the events of the swiftly flowing months that followed, as we have already indicated, merely seemed to confirm the belief of Phillips in the supremacy of the Democratic party led by the indomitable planting interest; events such as the downward revision of the tariff, the withdrawal of the ship subsidies, and the Dred Scott decision opening the territories to slavery.

All the while the conflict was growing more furious. Advocates of protection, taking advantage of the panic which followed the tariff revision, organized a stirring campaign to wean workingmen from their allegiance to a free-trade Democracy. Advocates of a sound currency protested against the depreciated notes and the wildcat banks that spread ruin through all sections of the land. The abolitionists maintained their fusillade, Garrison and Phillips, despite their pessimism, resting neither day nor night. Going beyond the bounds of mere agitation, the slavery faction of Missouri in its grim determination to conquer Kansas for bondage and northern abolitionists in their equally firm resolve to seize it for freedom convulsed the country by bloody deeds and then by bloody reprisals. In a powerful oration, "The Crime against Kansas," done in classical style but bristling with abuse of the slavery party, Charles Sumner threw Congress into a tumult in 1856 and provided a text for the free-soilers laboring to wrest the government from the planting interest. Before the public excitement caused by this speech had died away, the attention of the nation was arrested by a series of debates between Lincoln and Douglas held in Illinois in 1858 – debates which set forth in clear and logical form the program for excluding slavery from the territories and the squatter-sovereignty scheme for letting the inhabitants decide the issue for themselves.

Then came the appalling climax in 1859 when John Brown, after a stormy career in Kansas, tried to kindle a servile insurrection in the South. In the spring of that year, Brown attended an antislavery convention from which he went away muttering: "These men are all talk; what we need is action – action!" Collecting a few daring comrades he made a raid into Harper's Ferry for the purpose of starting a slave rebellion. Though his efforts failed, though he was quickly executed as a "traitor to Virginia," the act of violence rocked the continent from sea to sea.

In vain did the Republicans try to treat it as the mere work of a fanatic and denounce it as "among the gravest of crimes." In vain did Lincoln attempt to minimize it as an absurd adventure that resulted in nothing noteworthy except the death of Brown. It resounded through the land with the clangor of an alarm bell, aggravating the jangling nerves of a people already excited by fears of a race war and continued disturbances over the seizure of slaves under the fugitive slave act – disorders which sometimes assumed the form of menacing riots.

The turmoil in the country naturally found sharp echoes in the halls of Congress. Buchanan's policy of aiding the slavery party in its efforts to get possession of Kansas and the taunting action of the free-soilers in their determination to save it for liberty, gave abundant occasions for debates that grew more and more acrimonious. Indeed the factions in Congress were now almost at swords' points, passion in argument and gesture becoming the commonplace of the day.

When Senator Sumner made a vehement verbal attack on Senator Butler of

South Carolina in 1856, Preston Brooks, a Representative from the same state and a relative of the latter, replied in terms of physical force, catching Sumner unawares and beating his victim senseless with a heavy cane. Though the act was not strictly chivalrous – for Sumner, wedged in between his chair and his desk, could not defend himself – admiring South Carolinians gave Brooks a grand banquet and presented him with a new cane bearing the words: "Use knockdown arguments." On both sides of the Senate chamber all the arts of diplomacy were discarded, and the meanest weapons of personal abuse brought into play. Douglas called Sumner a perjurer who spat forth malignity upon his colleagues. The prim, proud Senator from Massachusetts, conscious of possessing a mellow culture, replied by likening Douglas to a "noisome, squat and nameless animal" that filled the Senate with an offensive odor.

Things were even worse in the lower house. Again and again debate was on the verge of physical combat, for which members equipped themselves with knives and revolvers. A Representative from Pennsylvania and another from North Carolina had to be put under bonds to keep the peace. A general mêlée occurred in the spring of 1860 when Lovejoy, whose brother had been shot by a pro-slavery mob in Illinois, made an unbridled attack on slave owners and Democrats, advanced to their side of the house shaking his fists in a terrible rage, and threw the whole chamber into such a confusion that all the resources of experienced leaders were needed to prevent bloodshed then and there. Without exaggeration did Jefferson Davis exclaim that members of Congress were more like the agents of belligerent states than men assembled in the interest of common welfare – an utterance that was startlingly accurate – born of prophetic certainty. After a few fleeting days, the irrepressible conflict that had so long been raging was actually to pass from the forum to the battlefield, to that court where the only argument was the sword and where the one answer that admitted of no appeal was death.

Every shocking incident on the one side only consolidated the forces on the other. By 1860 leaders of the planting interest had worked out in great detail their economic and political scheme – their ultimatum to the serried opposition – and embodied it in many official documents. The economic elements were those made familiar to the country through twenty years of agitation: no high protective tariffs, no ship subsidies, no national banking and currency system; in short, none of the measures which business enterprise deemed essential to its progress. The remaining problem before the planting interest, namely, how to clinch its grip and prevent a return to the Hamilton-Webster policy as the industrial North rapidly advanced in wealth and population, was faced with the same penchant for definition.

Plans for accomplishing that purpose were mapped out by able spokesmen from the South in a set of Senate resolutions adopted on May 24-25, 1860: slavery is lawful in all the territories under the Constitution; neither Congress nor a local legislature can abolish it there; the federal government is in duty bound to protect slave owners as well as the holders of other forms of property in the territories; it is a violation of the Constitution for any state or any combination of citizens to intermeddle with the domestic institutions of any other state "on any pretext whatever, political, moral, or religious, with a view to their disturbance or subversion"; open or covert attacks on slavery are contrary to the solemn pledges given by the states on entering the Union to protect and defend one another; the inhabitants of a territory on their admission to the Union may decide whether or not they will sanction slavery thereafter; the strict enforcement of the fugitive slave law is required by good faith and the principles of the Constitution.

In brief, the federal government was to do nothing for business enterprise while the planting interest was to be assured the possession of enough political power to guarantee it against the reënactment of the Hamilton-Webster program. Incidentally the labor system of the planting interest was not to be criticized and all runaway property was to be returned. Anything short of this was, in the view of the planting statesmen, "subversive of the Constitution."

The meaning of the ultimatum was not to be mistaken. It was a demand upon the majority of the people to surrender unconditionally for all time to the minority stockholders under the Constitution. It offered nothing to capitalism but capitulation; to the old Whigs of the South nothing but submission. Finally — and this was its revolutionary phase — it called upon the farmers and mechanics who had formed the bulk of Jacksonian Democracy in the North to acknowledge the absolute sovereignty of the planting interest. Besides driving a wedge into the nation, the conditions laid down by the planters also split the Democratic party itself into two factions.

Soon after the Democratic convention assembled at Charleston in April, 1860, this fundamental division became manifest. The northern wing, while entirely willing to indorse the general economic program of the planters, absolutely refused to guarantee them sovereignty in the party and throughout the country. Rejecting the proposal of the southern members to make slavery obligatory in the territories, it would merely offer to "abide by the decisions of the Supreme Court on all questions of constitutional law." Since the Dred Scott case had opened all the territories to slavery, that tender seemed generous enough but the intransigent representatives of the planting interest would not accept it as adequate. Unable to overcome the majority commanded in the convention by the northern group, they withdrew from the assembly, spurning the pleas of their colleagues not to break up the union of hearts on "a mere theory" and countering all arguments with a declaration of finality: "Go your way and we will go ours."

After balloting for a time on candidates without reaching a decision under the two-thirds rule, the remaining members of the Charleston conference adjourned to meet again at Baltimore. When they reassembled, they nominated Stephen A. Douglas of Illinois, the apostle of "squatter sovereignty," who was ready to open the territories to slavery but not to guarantee the planting interest unconditional supremacy in the Democratic party and the Union. Determined to pursue their separate course to the bitter end, the Charleston seceders adopted the platform rejected by the Douglas faction and chose as their candidate, John C. Breckinridge of Kentucky, an unyielding champion of planting aristocracy and its labor system. The union of farmers and slave owners was thus severed: the Republicans had carried off one large fragment of the northern farmers in 1856; Douglas was now carrying off another.

During the confusion in the Democratic ranks, the Republicans, in high glee over the quarrels of the opposition, held their convention in Chicago — a sectional gathering except for representatives from five slave states. Among its delegates the spirit of opposition to slavery extension, which had inspired the party assembly four years before, was still evident but enthusiasm on that ticklish subject was neutralized by the prudence of the practical politicians who, sniffing victory in the air, had rushed to the new tent. Whigs, whose affections were centered on Hamilton's program rather than on Garrison's scheme of salvation, were to be seen on the floor. Advocates of a high protective tariff and friends of free homesteads for mechanics and farmers now mingled with the ardent opponents of slavery in the territories. With their minds fixed on the substance of things sought for, the partisans of caution were almost able to prevent the convention from indorsing the Declaration of Independence. Still they were in favor of restricting the area of slavery; they had no love for the institution and its spread helped to fasten the grip of the planting interest on the government at Washington. So the Republican convention went on record in favor of liberty for the territories, free homesteads for farmers, a protective tariff, and a Pacific railway. As the platform was read, the cheering became especially loud and prolonged when the homestead and tariff planks were reached. Such at least is the testimony of the stenographic report.

Since this declaration of principles was well fitted to work a union of forces, it was essential that the candidate should not divide them. The protective plank would doubtless line up the good old Whigs of the East but tender consideration had to be shown to the Ohio Valley, original home of Jacksonian Democracy, where national banks, tariffs, and other "abominations" still frightened the wary. Without Ohio, Indiana, and Illinois, the Republican managers could not hope to win and they knew that the lower counties of these states were filled with settlers from the slave belt who had no love for the "money power," abolition, or anything that savored of them. In such circumstances Seward, idol of the Whig wing, was no man to offer that section; he was too radical on the slavery issue and too closely associated with "high finance" in addition. "If you do not nominate Seward, where will you get your money?" was the blunt question put by Seward's loyal supporters at Chicago. The question was pertinent but not fatal.

Given this confluence of problems, a man close to the soil of the West was better suited to the requirements of the hour than a New York lawyer with somewhat fastidious tastes, obviously backed by fat purses. The available candidate was Abraham Lincoln of Illinois. Born in Kentucky, he was of southern origin. A son of poor frontier parents, self-educated, a pioneer who in his youth had labored in field and forest, he appealed to the voters of the backwoods. Still by an uncanny genius for practical affairs, he had forged his way to the front as a shrewd lawyer and politician. In his debates with Douglas he had shown himself able to cope with one of the foremost leaders in the Democratic party. On the tariff, bank, currency, and homestead issues he was sound. A local railway attorney, he was trusted among business men.

On the slavery question Lincoln's attitude was firm but conservative. He disliked slavery and frankly said so; yet he was not an abolitionist and he saw no way in which the institution could be uprooted. On the contrary, he favored enforcing the fugitive slave law and he was not prepared to urge even the abolition of slavery in the District of Columbia. His declaration that a house divided against itself could not stand had been counterbalanced by an assertion that the country would become all free or all slave – a creed which any southern planter could have indorsed. Seward's radical doctrine that there was a "higher law" than the Constitution, dedicating the territories to freedom, received from the Illinois lawyer disapproval, not commendation.

Nevertheless Lincoln was definite and positive in his opinion that slavery should not be permitted in the territories. That was necessary to satisfy the minimum demands of the anti-slavery faction and incidentally it pleased those Whigs of the North who at last realized that no Hamiltonian program could be pushed through Congress if the planting interest secured a supremacy, or indeed held an equal share of power, in the Union. Evidently Lincoln was the man of the hour: his heritage was correct, his principles were sound, his sincerity was unquestioned, and his ability as a speaker commanded the minds and hearts of his auditors. He sent word to his friends at Chicago that, although he did not indorse Seward's higher-law doctrine, he agreed with him on the irrepressible conflict. The next day Lincoln was nominated amid huzzas from ten thousand lusty throats.

A large fraction of Whigs and some fragments of the Know Nothing, or American, party, foreseeing calamity in the existing array of interests, tried to save the day by an appeal to lofty sentiments without any definitions. Assuming the name of Constitutional Unionists and boasting that they represented the "intelligence and respectability of the South" as well as the lovers of the national idea everywhere, they held a convention at Baltimore and nominated John Bell of Tennessee and Edward Everett of Massachusetts for President and Vice-President. In the platform they invited their countrymen to forget all divisions and "support the Constitution of the country, the union of the states, and the enforcement of the laws." It was an overture of old men – men who had known and loved Webster and Clay and who shrank with horror from agitations that threatened to end in bloodshed and revolution – a plea for the maintenance of the status quo against the whims of a swiftly changing world.

A spirited campaign followed the nomination of these four candidates for the presidency on four different platforms. Huge campaign funds were raised and spent. Beside pursuing the usual strategy of education, the Republicans resorted to parades and the other spectacular features that had distinguished the log-cabin crusade of General Harrison's year. Emulating the discretion of the Hero of Tippecanoe, Lincoln maintained a judicious silence at Springfield while his champions waged his battles for him, naturally tempering their orations to the requirements of diverse interests. They were fully conscious, as a Republican paper in Philadelphia put it, that "Frémont had tried running on the slavery issue and lost." So while they laid stress on it in many sections, they widened their appeal.

In the West, a particular emphasis was placed on free homesteads and the Pacific railway. With a keen eye for competent strategy, Carl Schurz carried the campaign into Missouri where he protested with eloquence against the action of the slave power in denying "the laboring man the right to acquire property in the soil by his labor" and made a special plea for the German vote on the ground that the free land was to be opened to aliens who declared their intention of becoming American citizens. Discovering that the homestead question was "the greatest issue in the West," Horace Greeley used it to win votes in the East. Agrarians and labor reformers renewed the slogan: "Vote yourself a farm."

In Pennsylvania and New Jersey, protection for iron and steel was the great subject of discussion. Curtin, the Republican candidate for governor in the former state, said not a word about abolishing slavery in his ratification speech but spoke with feeling on "the vast heavings of the heart of Pennsylvania whose sons are pining for protection to their labor and their dearest interests." Warming to his theme, he exclaimed: "This is a contest involving protection and the rights of labor. . . . If you desire to become vast and great, protect the manufactures of Philadelphia. . . . All hail, liberty! All hail, freedom! freedom to the white man! All hail freedom general as the air we breathe!" In a fashion after Curtin's own heart, the editor of the Philadelphia American and Gazette, surveying the canvass at the finish, repudiated the idea that "any sectional aspect of the slavery question" was up for decision and declared that the great issues were protection for industry, "economy in the conduct of the government, homesteads for settlers on the public domain, retrenchment and accountability in the public expenditures, appropriation for rivers and harbors, a Pacific railroad, the admission of Kansas, and a radical reform in the government."

With a kindred appreciation of practical matters, Seward bore the standard through the North and West. Fully conversant with the Webster policy of commercial expansion in the Pacific and knowing well the political appeal of Manifest Destiny, he proclaimed the future of the American empire — assuring his auditors that in due time American outposts would be pushed along the northwest coast to the Arctic Ocean, that Canada would be gathered into our glorious Union, that the Latin-American republics reorganized under our benign influence would become parts of this magnificent confederation, that the ancient Aztec metropolis, Mexico City, would eventually become the capital of the United States, and that America and Russia, breaking their old friendship, would come to grips in the Far East — "in regions where civilization first began." All this was involved in the election of Lincoln and the triumph of the Republican party. Webster and Cushing and Perry had not wrought in vain.

The three candidates opposed to Lincoln scored points wherever they could. Douglas took the stump with his usual vigor and declaimed to throngs in nearly every state. Orators of the Breckinridge camp, believing that their extreme views were sound everywhere, invaded the North. Bell's champions spoke with dignity and warmth about the dangers inherent in all unwise departures from the past, about the perils of the sectional quarrel. When at length the ballots were cast and counted, it was found that the foes of slavery agitation had carried the country by an overwhelming majority. Their combined vote was a million ahead of Lincoln's total; the two Democratic factions alone, to say nothing of Bell's six hundred thousand followers, outnumbered the Republican army. But in the division and uproar of the campaign Lincoln, even so, had won the Presidency; he was the choice of a minority —a sectional minority at that — but under the terms of the Constitution, he was entitled to the scepter at Washington.

From what has just been said it must be apparent that the forces which produced the irrepressible conflict were very complex in nature and yet the momentous struggle has been so often reduced by historians to simple terms that a reexamination of the traditional thesis has become one of the tasks of the modern age. On the part of northern writers it was long the fashion to declare that slavery was the cause of the conflict between the states. Such for example was the position taken by James Ford Rhodes and made the starting point of his monumental work.

Assuming for the moment that this assertion is correct in a general sense, it will be easily observed even on a superficial investigation that "slavery" was no simple, isolated phenomenon. In itself it was intricate and it had filaments through the whole body economic. It was a labor system, the basis of planting, and the foundation of the southern aristocracy. That aristocracy, in turn, owing to the nature of its economic operations, resorted to public policies that were opposed to capitalism, sought to dominate the federal government, and, with the help of free farmers also engaged in agriculture, did at last dominate it. In the course of that political conquest, all the plans of commerce and industry for federal protection and subvention were overborne. It took more than a finite eye to discern where slavery as an ethical question left off and economics — the struggle over the distribution of wealth — began.

On the other hand, the early historians of the southern school, chagrined by defeat and compelled to face the adverse judgment of brutal fact, made the "rights of states" — something nobler than economics or the enslavement of Negroes — the issue for which the Confederacy fought and bled. That too like slavery seems simple until subjected to a little scrutiny. What is a state? At bottom it is a majority or perhaps a mere plurality of persons engaged in the quest of something supposed to be beneficial, or at all events not injurious, to the pursuers. And what are rights? Abstract, intangible moral values having neither substance nor form? The party debates over the economic issues of the middle period answer with an emphatic negative. If the southern planters had been content to grant tariffs, bounties, subsidies, and preferences to northern commerce and industry, it is not probable that they would have been molested in their most imperious proclamations of sovereignty.

But their theories and their acts involved interests more ponderable than political rhetoric. They threatened the country with secession first in defying the tariff of abominations and when they did secede thirty years later it was in response to the victory of a tariff and homestead party that proposed nothing more dangerous to slavery itself than the mere exclusion of the institution from the territories. It took more than a finite eye to discern where their opposition to the economic system of Hamilton left off and their affection for the rights of states began. The modern reader tossed about in a contrariety of opinions can only take his bearings by examining a few indubitable realities.

With reference to the popular northern view of the conflict, there stands the stubborn fact that at no time during the long gathering of the storm did Garrison's abolition creed rise to the dignity of a first rate political issue in the North.

Nobody but agitators, beneath the contempt of the towering statesmen of the age, ever dared to advocate it. No great political organization even gave it the most casual indorsement.

When the abolitionists launched the Liberty party in the campaign of 1844 to work for emancipation, as we have noted, the voters answered their plea for "the restoration of equality of political rights among men" in a manner that demonstrated the invincible opposition of the American people. Out of more than two and a half million ballots cast in the election, only sixty-five thousand were recorded in favor of the Liberty candidate. That was America's answer to the call for abolition; and the advocates of that policy never again ventured to appeal to the electorate by presenting candidates on such a radical platform.

No other party organized between that time and the clash of arms attempted to do more than demand the exclusion of slavery from the territories and not until the Democrats by repealing the Missouri Compromise threatened to extend slavery throughout the West did any party poll more than a handful of votes on that issue. It is true that Van Buren on a free-soil platform received nearly three hundred thousand votes in 1848 but that was evidently due to personal influence, because his successor on a similar ticket four years afterward dropped into an insignificant place.

Even the Republican party, in the campaign of 1856, coming hard on the act of defiance which swept away the Missouri compact, won little more than one-third the active voters to the cause of restricting the slavery area. When transformed after four more years into a homestead and high tariff party pledged merely to liberty in the territories, the Republicans polled a million votes fewer than the number cast for the opposing factions and rode into power on account of the divided ranks of the enemy. Such was the nation's reply to the anti-slavery agitation from the beginning of the disturbance until the cannon shot at Sumter opened a revolution.

Moreover not a single responsible statesman of the middle period committed himself to the doctrine of immediate and unconditional abolition to be achieved by independent political action. John Quincy Adams, ousted from the presidency by Jacksonian Democracy but returned to Washington as the Representative of a Massachusetts district in Congress, did declare that it was the duty of every free American to work directly for the abolition of slavery and with uncanny vision foresaw that the knot might be cut with the sword. But Adams was regarded by astute party managers as a foolish and embittered old man and his prophecy as a dangerous delusion.

Practical politicians who felt the iron hand of the planters at Washington — politicians who saw how deeply intertwined with the whole economic order the institution of slavery really was — could discover nothing tangible in immediate and unconditional abolition that appealed to reason or came within the range of common sense. Lincoln was emphatic in assuring the slaveholders that no Republican had ever been detected in any attempt to disturb them. "We must not interfere with the institution of slavery in the states where it exists," he urged, "because the Constitution forbids it and the general welfare does not require us to do so."

Since, therefore, the abolition of slavery never appeared in the platform of any great political party, since the only appeal ever made to the electorate on that issue was scornfully repulsed, since the spokesman of the Republicans emphatically declared that his party never intended to interfere with slavery in the states in any shape or form, it seems reasonable to assume that the institution of slavery was not the fundamental issue during the epoch preceding the bombardment of Fort Sumter.

Nor can it be truthfully said, as southern writers were fond of having it, that a tender and consistent regard for the rights of states and for a strict construction of the Constitution was the prime element in the dispute that long divided the country. As a matter of record, from the foundation of the republic, all factions were for high nationalism or low provincialism upon occasion according to their desires at the moment, according to turns in the balance of power. New England nullified federal law when her commerce was affected by the War of 1812 and came out stanchly for liberty and union, one and inseparable, now and forever, in 1833 when South Carolina attempted to nullify a tariff act. Not long afterward, the legislature of Massachusetts, dreading the overweening strength of the Southwest, protested warmly against the annexation of Texas and resolved that "such an act of admission would have no binding force whatever on the people of Massachusetts."

Equally willing to bend theory to practical considerations, the party of the slavocracy argued that the Constitution was to be strictly and narrowly construed whenever tariff and bank measures were up for debate; but no such piddling concept of the grand document was to be held when a bill providing for the prompt and efficient return of fugitive slaves was on the carpet. Less than twenty years after South Carolina prepared to resist by arms federal officers engaged in collecting customs duties, the champions of slavery and states' rights greeted with applause a fugitive slave law which flouted the precious limitations prescribed in the first ten Amendments to the Constitution – a law which provided for the use of all the powers of the national government to assist masters in getting possession of their elusive property – which denied to the alleged slave, who might perchance be a freeman in spite of his color, the right to have a jury trial or even to testify in his own behalf. In other words, it was "constitutional" to employ the engines of the federal authority in catching slaves wherever they might be found in any northern community and to ignore utterly the elementary safeguards of liberty plainly and specifically imposed on Congress by language that admitted of no double interpretation.

On this very issue of personal liberty, historic positions on states' rights were again reversed. Following the example of South Carolina on the tariff, Wisconsin resisted the fugitive slave law as an invasion of her reserved rights – as a violation of the Constitution. Alarmed by this action, Chief Justice Taney answered the disobedient state in a ringing judicial decision announcing a high nationalism that would have delighted the heart of John Marshall, informing the recalcitrant Wisconsin that the Constitution and laws enacted under it were supreme; that the fugitive slave law was fully authorized by the Constitution; and that the Supreme Court was the final arbiter in all controversies over the respective powers of the states and the United States. "If such an arbiter had not been provided in our complicated system of government, internal tranquillity could not have been preserved and if such controversies were left to the arbitrament of physical force, our Government, State and National, would cease to be a government of laws, and revolution by force of arms would take the place of courts of justice and judicial decisions." No nullification here; no right of a state to judge for itself respecting infractions of the Constitution by the federal government; federal law is binding everywhere and the Supreme Court, a branch of the national government, is the final judge.

And in what language did Wisconsin reply? The legislature of the state, in a solemn resolution, declared that the decision of the Supreme Court of the United States in the case in question was in direct conflict with the Constitution. It vowed that the essential principles of the Kentucky doctrine of nullification were sound. Then it closed with the rebel fling: "that the several states . . . being sovereign and independent, have the unquestionable right to judge of its [the Constitution's] infraction and that a positive defiance by those sovereignties of all unauthorized acts done or attempted to be done under color of that instrument is the rightful remedy."

That was in 1859. Within two years, men who had voted for that resolution and cheered its adoption were marching off in martial array to vindicate on southern battlefields the supremacy of the Union and the sovereignty of the nation. By that fateful hour the southern politicians who had applauded Taney's declaration that the Supreme Court was the final arbiter in controversies between the states and the national government had come to the solemn conclusion that the states themselves were the arbiters. Such words and events being facts, there can be but one judgment in the court of history; namely, that major premises respecting the nature of the Constitution and deductions made logically from them with masterly eloquence were minor factors in the grand dispute as compared with the interests, desires, and passions that lay deep in the hearts and minds of the contestants.

Indeed, honorable men who held diametrically opposite views found warrant for each in the Constitution. All parties and all individuals, save the extreme abolitionists, protested in an unbroken chant their devotion to the national covenant and to the principles and memory of the inspired men who framed it. As the Bible was sometimes taken as a guide for theologians traveling in opposite directions, so the Constitution was the beacon that lighted the way of statesmen who differed utterly on the issues of the middle period. Again and again Calhoun declared that his one supreme object was to sustain the Constitution in its pristine purity of principle: "to turn back the government," as he said, "to where it commenced its operation in 1789 . . . to take a fresh start, a new departure, on the States Rights Republican tack, as was intended by the framers of the Constitution."

This was the eternal refrain of Calhoun's school. The bank, subsidies to shipping, protection for industries, the encouragement of business enterprise by public asistance were all departures from the Constitution and the intentions of its framers, all contrary to the fundamental compact of the land. This refrain reverberated through Democratic speeches in Congress, the platform of the party, and the official utterances of its statesmen. "The liberal principles embodied by Jefferson in the Declaration of Independence and sanctioned by the Constitution . . . have ever been cardinal principles in the Democratic faith"— such was the characteristic declaration of the elect in every platform after 1840. The Constitution warrants the peaceful secession of states by legal process — such was the answer of Jefferson Davis to those who charged him with raising the flag of revolution. Everything done by the Democratic party while in power was constitutional and finally, as a crowning act of grace, the Constitution gave approval to its own destruction and the dissolution of the Union.

It followed from this line of reasoning as night the day that the measures advanced by the Whigs and later by the Republicans were unconstitutional. In fact, Calhoun devoted the burden of a great speech in 1839 to showing how everything done by Hamilton and his school was a violation of the Constitution. Party manifestoes reiterated the pronouncements of party statesmen on this point. In their platform of 1840, the Democrats highly resolved that "the Constitution does not confer upon the general government the power . . . to carry on a general system of internal improvement . . . the Constitution does not confer authority upon the federal government, directly or indirectly, to assume the debts of the several states . . . Congress has no power to charter a United States Bank . . . Congress has no power, under the Constitution, to interfere with or control the domestic institutions of the several states." This declaration was repeated every four years substantially in the same form. After the Supreme Court announced in the Dred Scott case that Congress could not prohibit slavery in the territories, the Democratic party added that the doctrine "should be respected by all good citizens and enforced with promptness and fidelity by every branch of the general government."

In the best of all possible worlds everything substantial desired by the Democrats was authorized by the Constitution while everything substantial opposed by them was beyond the boundaries set by the venerable instrument. Hamilton, who helped to draft the Constitution, therefore, did not understand or interpret it correctly; whereas Jefferson, who was in Paris during its formation was the infallible oracle on the intentions of its framers.

On the other hand, the Whigs and then the Republicans were equally prone to find protection under the ægis of the Constitution. Webster in his later years devoted long and eloquent speeches to showing that the Constitution contemplated a perpetual union and that nullification and secession were utterly proscribed by the principles of that instrument. He did not go as far as Calhoun. He did not declare free trade unconstitutional but he did find in the records of history evidence that "the main reason for the adoption of the Constitution" was to give "the general government the power to regulate commerce and trade." A protective tariff was therefore constitutional. Furthermore "it was no more the right than the duty" of Congress "by just discrimination to protect the labor of the American people." The provision of a uniform system of currency was also among "the chief objects" of the Fathers in framing the Constitution. A national bank was not imperatively commanded by the letter of the document but its spirit required Congress to stabilize and make sound the paper currency of the land. In fact Webster thought the Democrats themselves somewhat unconstitutional. "If by democracy," he said, "they mean a conscientious and stern adherence to the Constitution and the government, then I think they have very little claim to it."

In the endless and tangled debates on slavery, the orators of the age also paid the same sincere homage to the Constitution that they had paid when dealing with other economic matters. Southern statesmen on their side never wearied in pointing out the pro-slavery character of the covenant. That instrument, they said, recognized the slave trade by providing that the traffic should not be prohibited for twenty years and by leaving the issue open after that period had elapsed. It made slavery the basis of taxation and representation, "thus preferring and fostering it above all other property, by making it alone, of all property, an element of political power in the union, as well as a source of revenue to the federal government." The Constitution laid a binding obligation upon all states to return fugitive slaves to their masters upon claims made in due course. It guaranteed the states against domestic violence, not overlooking the possibilities of a servile revolt. "Power to abolish, circumscribe, or restrain slavery is withheld but power is granted and the duty is imposed on the federal government to protect and preserve it." The English language could hardly be more explicit.

All this was no accident; it was the outcome of design. "The framers of the Constitution were slave owners or the representatives of slave owners"; the Constitution was the result of a compromise between the North and the South in which slavery was specifically and zealously guarded and secured. Such were the canons of authenticity on the southern side.

This view of the Constitution contained so much sound historical truth that the opposition was forced to strain the imagination in its search for an answer. In an attempt to find lawful warrant for their creed in 1844, the abolitionists made a platform that became one of the prime curiosities in the annals of logic. They announced that the principles of the Declaration of Independence were embraced in the Constitution, that those principles proclaimed freedom, and that the provision of the Constitution relative to the return of fugitive slaves was itself null and void because forsooth common law holds any contract contrary to natural right and morality invalid.

Although the Republicans did not go that far in their defensive romancing, they also asserted, in their platform of 1860, that the principles of the Declaration of Independence were embodied in the Constitution and they claimed that neither Congress nor a state legislature could give legal existence to slavery in any territory of the United States. But there was one slip in this reasoning: the Supreme Court of the United States, with reference to the Dred Scott case, had read in the same oracle that Congress could not deprive any slave owner of his property in the territories and that the abolition of slavery there by Congress was null and void.

Nevertheless, the Republicans neatly evaded this condemnation of their doctrine, by calling it "a dangerous political heresy, at variance with the explicit provisions of that instrument itself, with contemporaneous exposition, and with legislative and judicial precedent." In short, the Republicans entered a dissenting opinion themselves; while it was hardly authentic constitutional law it made an effective appeal to voters — especially those fond of legal proprieties.

Even in their violent disagreement as to the nature of the Union, the contestants with equal fervor invoked the authority of the Constitution to show that secession was lawful or that the perpetuation of the Union was commanded as the case might be. With respect to this problem each party to the conflict had a theory which was finely and logically drawn from pertinent data and given the appearance of soundness by a process of skillful elision and emphasis.

Those who to-day look upon that dispute without rancor must admit that the secessionists had somewhat the better of the rhetorical side of the battle. Their scheme of historicity was simple. The thirteen colonies declared their independence as separate sovereignties; they were recognized by Great Britain in the treaty of peace as thirteen individual states; when they formed the Articles of Confederation they were careful to declare that "each state retains its sovereignty, freedom, and independence and every power, jurisdiction, and right, which is not by this Confederation expressly delegated to the United States in Congress assembled." These were undeniable facts. Then came the formation of the Constitution. The states elected delegates to the federal convention; the delegates revised the Articles of Confederation; the revision, known as the Constitution, was submitted for approval to the states and finally ratified by state conventions.

Q. E. D., ran the secessionist argument, the sovereign states that entered the compact can by lawful process withdraw from the Union just as sovereign nations may by their own act dissolve a treaty with other foreign powers.

There was, of course, some difficulty in discovering attributes of sovereignty in the new states carved out of the national domain by the surveyors' compass and chain and admitted to the Union under specific constitutional limitations – states that now outnumbered the original thirteen. But the slight hiatus in the argument, which arose from this incongruity, was bridged by the declaration that the subject territories when taken in under the roof were clothed with the sovereignty and independence of the original commonwealths.

The historical brief of those who maintained, on the other hand, that secession was illegal rested in part on an interpretation of the preamble of the Constitution, an interpretation advanced by Webster during his famous debate with Hayne. "It cannot be shown," he said, "that the Constitution is a compact between state governments. The Constitution itself, in its very front, refutes that idea; it declares that it is ordained and established by the people of the United States. . . . It even does not say that it is established by the people of the several states; but pronounces that it is established by the the people of the United States in the aggregate." That is, the Constitution was not made by the states; it was made by a high collective sovereign towering above them – the people of the United States.

This fair argument, which seemed convincing on its face, was later demolished by reference to the journals of the Convention that drafted the Constitution. When the preamble was originally drawn, it ran: "We, the people of the states of New Hampshire, Massachusetts, &c., . . . do ordain and establish the following Constitution." But on second thought the framers realized that according to their own decree the new government was to be set up as soon as nine states had ratified the proposed instrument. It was obviously undesirable to enumerate the states of the Union in advance, for some of them might withhold their approval. Therefore the first draft was abandoned and the words "We the people of the United States" substituted. The facts of record accordingly exploded the whole thesis built on this sandy foundation.

This fallacy Lincoln was careful to avoid in his first inaugural address. Seeking a more secure historical basis for his faith, he pointed out that the Union was in fact older than the Constitution, older than the Declaration of Independence. It was formed, he said, by the Articles of Association framed in 1774 by the Continental Congress speaking in the name of revolutionary America. It was matured and continued in the Declaration of Independence which proclaimed "these United Colonies" to be free and independent states. It was sealed by the Articles of Confederation which pledged the thirteen commonwealths to a perpetual Union under that form of government; it was crowned by the Constitution designed to make the Union "more perfect."

Far more effective on the nationalist side was the argument derived through logical processes from the nature of the Constitution itself, by Webster, Lincoln, and the philosophers of their school. It ran in the following vein. The Constitution does not, by express provision or by implication, provide any method by which a state may withdraw from the Union; no such dissolution of the federation was contemplated by the men who drafted and ratified the covenant. The government established by it operates directly on the people, not on states; it is the government of the people, not of states. Moreover the Constitution proclaims to all the world that it and the laws and treaties made in pursuance of its terms, are the supreme law of the land and that the judges of the states are bound thereby, "anything in the constitution and laws of any state to the contrary notwithstanding." Finally, the Supreme Court of the United States is the ultimate arbiter in all controversies arising between the national government and the states. Chief Justice Marshall had proclaimed the doctrine in beating down the resistance of Virginia, Maryland, and Ohio to federal authority; Chief Justice Taney had proclaimed it in paralyzing the opposition of Wisconsin to the fugitive slave law. Such being the grand pledges and principles of the Constitution it followed, to use Lincoln's version, that no state could lawfully withdraw from the Union; secession was insurrectionary or revolutionary according to circumstances.

What now is the verdict of history on these verbal contests? Did the delegates at the Philadelphia convention of 1787 regard themselves as ambassadors of sovereign states entering into a mere treaty of alliance? Did they set down anywhere a pontifical judgment to the effect that any state might on its own motion withdraw from the Union after approving the Constitution? The answer to these questions is in the negative. Had they thought out a logical system of political theory such as Calhoun afterward announced with such precision? If so, they left no record of it to posterity.

What then was the Constitution? It was a plan of government designed to effect certain purposes, specific and general, framed by a small group of citizens, "informed by a conscious solidarity of interests," who, according to all available evidence, intended that government to be supreme over the states and enduring. They were not dominated by any logical scheme such as Calhoun evolved in defending his cause; they were engrossed in making, not breaking, a Union; they made no provision for, and if the testimony of their recorded debates be accepted as conclusive, did not contemplate the withdrawal of the states from the federation by any legal procedure. Surely it was not without significance that James Madison, the father of the Constitution, who lived to see secession threatened in South Carolina, denounced in unmistakable terms the smooth and well-articulated word-pattern of Calhoun, condemning secession as utterly without support in the understandings of the men who made, ratified, and launched the Constitution.

But it may be said that the men of Philadelphia merely drafted the Constitution and that what counts in the premises is the opinions of the voters in the states, who through their delegates ratified the instrument. Did, then, the men who chose the delegates for the state ratifying conventions or the delegates themselves have clearly in mind a concept that made the great document in effect a mere treaty of alliance which could be legally denounced at will by any member? The records in the case give no affirmative answer. What most of them thought is a matter of pure conjecture. Were any of the states sovereign in fact at any time; that is, did any of them assume before the world the attributes and functions of a sovereign nation? Certainly not. Did the whole people in their collective capacity make the Constitution? To ask the question is to answer it; they did not.

When the modern student examines all the verbal disputes over the nature of the Union – the arguments employed by the parties which operated and opposed the federal government between the adoption of the Constitution and the opening of the Civil War – he can hardly do otherwise than conclude that the linguistic devices used first on one side and then on the other were not derived from inherently necessary concepts concerning the intimate essence of the federal system. The roots of the controversy lay elsewhere – in social groupings founded on differences in climate, soil, industries, and labor systems, in divergent social forces, rather than varying degrees of righteousness and wisdom, or what romantic historians call "the magnetism of great personalities."

Philip S. Foner: BUSINESS AND SLAVERY

MUCH has been written concerning the causes of the Civil War in America since 1866, when Horace Greeley completed his *American Conflict*, and Edward A. Pollard published his *Lost Cause: A New Southern History of the War of the Confederates.* But in few of the many volumes devoted to this subject has there yet appeared an examination of the reactions of Northern business men to the conflict between the North and the South. This, no doubt, is due partly to the belief that slavery and states'-rights were the sole questions worthy of consideration. But it is also due to an over-simplified economic interpretation of the causes of the Civil War. As presented most ably by Charles A. Beard in *The Rise of American Civilization,* this interpretation explains the war as the result of a conflict between two divergent economies, one an undiversified agrarian economy based on slavery, the other a commercial, industrial, financial, and diversified agricultural economy based on free labor. Northern business men, according to this interpretation, allied themselves with laborers and farmers to drive the planter aristocracy of the South from power in the government.

In breaking from the traditional thesis that the Civil War resulted only from a struggle over slavery, Professor Beard contributed much of great value to American historiography. But this should not obscure the fact that this distinguished historian because of the novelty of his thesis, tended to over-simplify it. Undoubtedly there were business men in the North who participated in movements which sought to dethrone the Southern planters from control of the national government. But it is also true that many Northern business men were intimately tied by social and economic bonds to the Southern planters. As a consequence, they allied themselves frequently with the planters to halt the growth of movements which waged a bitter struggle against the system of slavery, and which urged the ousting of the planters from their control of the national government. These business men feared the dissolution of the Union and the disruption of trade relations with the South more than they disliked slavery and more than they resented the control of the national government by the planter aristocrats.

Nowhere was this more evident than in New York City, the nation's leading commercial and financial center. Moreover, although the reactions of New York business men to the sectional dispute are probably not in every respect typical of those experienced by other Northern business men, the foregoing story of these reactions, from the beginning of the sectional struggle until the outbreak of civil war, reveals how difficult it is to regard the war as the result of a pure and simple conflict between two opposing economies.

The early chapters of this story have attempted to make clear a conflict that existed in the minds of these business men. On the one hand, they desired to restore tranquility to a troubled nation, but on the other, they also wished to prevent the expansion of what they termed "the alarming evil of slavery." Before the sectional struggle had assumed the proportions of a major issue which threatened to disrupt the economic relations between the North and South, the merchants had frequently indicated distinct hostility to the further extension of slavery. As early as 1819, at the time of the controversy over the Tallmadge amendment, the business men had recorded their resolution to oppose the existence of human bondage in "the states and territories hereafter to be organized in the wide domain of the United States." They maintained this stand for thirty years. In 1844 they opposed the annexation of Texas, and, four years later, they endorsed the Wilmot Proviso and urged the defeat of all compromise proposals which entailed the "surrender of an inch of free-soil to slavery."

Gradually, most merchants retreated from this position. By the end of the next decade, they not only affirmed the right of the planters to take their slaves into any and all territories of the United States, but they even asserted that it was the duty of the Federal government to protect slavery in these areas.

What forces caused this remarkable change?

First and foremost, the merchants were men of business. As such, they had most to lose by sectional disputes which interrupted the flow of trade between the North and South. Hence, when it appeared to them that politicians and fanatics, by clamor and propaganda, were utilizing the very principles they had endorsed for the purpose of widening the sectional breach, they determined to abandon these principles. Thus in 1850, when the merchants believed that the Wilmot Proviso, which they had hitherto supported, was being employed by agitators to create a political crisis that endangered the Union, they relinquished the proviso and fought for the compromise measure. In 1855, when they were convinced that the repeal of the Missouri Compromise, an action which they had bitterly attacked, was aiding the growth of a sectional party, they lost interest in this question and organized to defeat Republican candidates. Three years later, when they felt that the battle over the Lecompton Constitution was serving a similar purpose, they swallowed their distaste for the frauds involved in the adoption of that document and supported Buchanan's policy in the belief that it would remove the Kansas issue from national politics. Finally, at the time of the secession crisis, when political leaders hesitated to grant important concessions to the South, the merchants bombarded Congress with memorials calling for the adoption of compromise proposals which would guarantee protection of slavery in all territories of the United States.

Owing to their trade connections with the South, the merchants were, throughout the entire ante bellum period, in an excellent position to gauge accurately the sentiments of the Southerners. They were, therefore, more than any other group in the North, aware of the necessity of convincing the Southerners that the North did not, as many of them believed, consist only of people who were bitterly hostile to Southern institutions and who were bent upon interfering with Southern rights. Hence, the merchants were always the first to conduct Union meetings, at which they demonstrated their support for principles which Southerners cherished. These meetings were carefully reported in Southern newspapers; and were often influential in the victories scored by the Union forces in the South.

But meetings, the business men soon discovered, were not enough. Even though they adopted resolutions to dispel Southern apprehensions, radicals, gaining positions of political power, were soon able to undo the effects of scores of Union meetings. Therefore, the merchants concluded, these politicians had to be ousted from power and replaced by Union men who knew no North or South. Then, when the agitators had been silenced, and the voice of the North would speak through Union demonstrations, domestic peace would be restored, the slavery question would be pushed into the background, and economic and financial reforms, so essential for business prosperity, would receive proper consideration at the hands of legislators.

In quest of this goal, the vast majority of the merchants devoted much of their time and a good deal of their private funds for more than a decade to the task of defeating politicians whom they regarded as enemies of the Union. Frequently they were successful. In 1851, by sponsoring a Union state ticket, they defeated several anti-Compromise candidates, and elected conservatives. A year later, they played a major role in the defeat of Winfield Scott for the presidency, and rejoiced that this was a decisive blow to Sewardism. In the next presidential election, the merchants not only helped carry New York for Buchanan, but by means of their financial contributions, they also aided in his victory in Pennsylvania. Four years later, they were less successful, but even then they were responsible for the fact that Lincoln lost the Empire City.

Not all New York business men, however, united in these activities. A small but influential group of merchants joined the ranks of the Republicans, believing that peace and prosperity would never be achieved under administrations dominated by Southerners. They felt that it was futile to shout for Union and compromise as long as slaveholders and their Northern allies broke agreement after agreement, defied Northern opinion, and engaged in fraudulent practices to maintain power. They were convinced that the election of a Republican president would be a triumph for conservatism, for they believed that the fire-eaters of the South, with threats of secession, with recourse to political and economic intimidation, were truly the ones responsible for sectional dissensions. Finally, the business men were of the opinion that an administration dominated by Southerners would be forced to neglect measures essential for the prosperity of Northern business. Only a Republican president would and could offer solutions for the many defects within the business system.

But though these two groups of merchants differed over the means of achieving domestic peace, they were as one in their desire to save the Union. For, regardless of their political views, all business men, especially in the years following the panic of 1857, benefited from their Southern trade connections, and during the panic following Lincoln's election, all suffered severely. Hence, it was logical that all business men should have united during the secession crisis to urge Congress to adopt a compromise policy which would preserve the Union peacefully, and that they should have joined together on numerous delegations to exert influence on Washington for that purpose.

It was also exceedingly logical that when all efforts to save the Union peacefully had failed, the merchants, regardless of political views, should have endorsed the recourse to an armed policy. They had conducted their long struggle to prevent the dissolution of the Union because they knew that their very existence as business men depended upon the outcome. When they finally became aware of the economic chaos secession was causing, when they saw the entire business system crumbling before their very eyes, they knew that there was no choice left. The Union must be preserved. Any other outcome meant economic suicide.

It may be well to point out again, in closing this study, that the course taken by the New York merchants during the months preceding and following the fall of Fort Sumter, exercised a significant influence over national affairs. By their control of finances, the business men compelled Buchanan to take a firm stand toward the secessionists. By their delegations and memorials, they gave considerable influence to the movement to secure a peaceful settlement of the difficulties, and they helped in their interviews with members of Congress to keep the border state delegates from joining the secessionists. Finally, when the war was begun by the confederate states, the merchants, by their zeal and financial aid, enabled the government to conduct an efficient campaign for the extension of the political and economic authority of the United States over all parts of the country.

Thus it came about that the efforts of New York business men to save the Union by concession, compromise and surrender evolved logically into an intransigent determination to prosecute a great civil war to a victorious conclusion.

Rollin G. Osterweis: SOUTH CAROLINA AND THE IDEA OF SOUTHERN NATIONALISM

"At last we are a nation among nations."
HENRY TIMROD, South Carolina poet, February, 1861

THE idea of Southern nationalism, which developed chiefly in South Carolina during the decade before the Civil War, was the most ambitious romantic manifestation of the antebellum period. It is not unnatural that this energy-demanding and forward-looking trend should have been cradled in a hard-headed community. These were people anxious to lead – possessing political and intellectual talent, accumulated wealth, influential periodicals, and a past history of fiery, independent thinking. Around 1850 the Cotton Kingdom was looking for leadership; and the Palmetto State stood ready to fill that need. It was soon ahead of the times, waiting for the rest of the South to catch up with its daring plans.

The State of South Carolina, and the city of Charleston, were peculiarly well suited to lead the revolt toward separate Southern nationality. As Frederick Jackson Turner has pointed out, Charleston was the one important center of city life on the Atlantic seaboard below Baltimore. Every February planters from a radius of several hundred miles would gather for a month in their Charleston town houses; during the summer, the threat of malaria in the country would bring many of them back again. While in town, they mingled with informed people from other sections of the South, and from the North as well. Their wide range of experience in plantation management, mercantile activity, and political life gave them powerful advantages for leadership.[1]

From the administration of Washington through that of Monroe, the tobacco planters of Virginia had ruled not only the South but, under the presidential dynasty, the nation itself. In the late 1820's, the center of power, below the Mason and Dixon line, was passing from the hands of Virginia to those of South Carolina. And, at the same time, the South as a unit was beginning to realize that it was becoming a minority section. The rapid growth of the cotton area was fixing slavery as a permanent and expanding institution and slavery was setting the section apart from the rest of the United States. When Northeast and Northwest tended to unite in fostering protective tariffs and internal improvement programs, which deprived the cotton states of their profits to enhance an industrial

[1] Frederick Jackson Turner, *Rise of the New West*, in "The American Nation" series, Albert Bushnell Hart, ed. (27 vols., New York, Harper and Brothers, 1904–1908), XIV, 63.

structure of no benefit to them, blood ran hot in Carolina.[2]

The idea of Southern nationalism emerged about 1850 out of an experience mainly native and nonromantic. During the ten years before the war, it took on a distinctive, romantic coloration. It lay rooted in the adventures of the American colonies themselves in 1776; in the Lockian philosophy of Thomas Cooper; in familiarity with the political devices suggested by the onetime American nationalist, John C. Calhoun; in the Tariff and Nullification episode between 1827 and 1833; in the problems produced by the territorial acquisitions of the Mexican war; in the various Southern economic conventions, down to and including the historic Nashville meeting of November, 1850. By the latter year, certainly, a group consciousness had developed, an *ethnocentrism,* an impulse for Southern nationalism. The impulse was so similar to the ideas of romantic nationalism, then prevalent in Europe, that it offered a natural affinity for those ideas.

The leadership for the translation of this impulse into action would come first from a group of South Carolinians, headed by Senator Barnwell, A. P. Butler, and the elder Langdon Cheves. Later, others would take up the torch.

It is highly significant to note that, although he does not use the term "romantic Southern nationalism," Edward Channing calls the sixth volume of his history, *The War for Southern Independence, 1849–1865;* and opens that volume with excerpts from the speech of Langdon Cheves, Southern nationalist of South Carolina, at the Nashville convention, November 14, 1850.[3] Channing interprets the crusade for separate Southern nationality as starting around 1849. In doing so he draws particular attention to Cheves of Carolina and to what he said at Nashville.[4]

Launching his attack on Clay's compromise measures, known collectively as the Omnibus Bill, the aged Cheves had declared:

> In nine months, in one session of Congress, by a great *coup d'état,* our Constitution has been completely and forever subverted. . . . What is the remedy? I answer: secession — united secession of the slave-holding States. . . . Nothing else will be wise — nothing else will be practicable. . . . Unite, and you shall form one of the most splendid empires on which the sun ever shone, of the most homogeneous population, all of the same blood and lineage, a soil the most fruitful, and a climate the most lovely. . . . O, Great God, unite us, and a tale of submission shall never be told.[5]

Channing is at considerable pains to point out that this concept of a "homogeneous population, all of the same blood and lineage," was far removed from the actualities of the 1850 Southland. He notes that Charleston itself was a heterogeneous medley of English, French, Scotch-Irish, Germans, Portuguese Jews, Irish Catholics, and Welsh. In another part of his speech, Cheves had asserted that the Southerners were "all of gentle descent," and Channing demolishes this exaggeration with breath-taking effectiveness.[6]

There is a pertinent conclusion to be drawn from all this, namely, that Lang-

[2] *Ibid.*, pp. 50–63.

[3] Edward Channing, *A History of the United States, 1000–1865,* VI, 1.

[4] *Ibid.*, VI, 1, 82–84.

[5] Ulrich B. Phillips, "The Literary Movement for Secession," *Studies in Southern History and Politics* (New York, 1914), pp. 42–44. Cheves's speech is given more fully here than in Channing.

[6] Channing, *op. cit.*, VI, 6–12.

don Cheves, ardent Southern nationalist, was expressing the very essence of romantic nationalism at Nashville in November, 1850. Romantic nationalism, in the contemporary framework of reference, was cultural nationalism, and that is what Cheves was talking about – the longing of a "homogeneous population, all of the same blood and lineage," and possessing common institutions for national existence. The fact that this racial homogeneity was a myth, but passionately believed to be true, deepens the romantic coloring.

The Carolinian conviction that Southerners comprised a separate cultural unit grew stronger from the concomitant belief that the rest of the country possessed an inferior civilization. So obvious was this attitude by 1860 that the correspondent of the London *Times* could grasp it completely. In a letter dated "Charleston, April 30, 1861," William Howard Russell declared:

> Believe a Southern man as he believes himself and you must regard New England and the kindred states as the birthplace of impurity of mind among men and of unchastity in women – the home of Free Love, of Fourierism, of Infidelity, of Abolitionism, of false teachings in political economy and in social life; a land saturated with the drippings of rotten philosophy, with the poisonous infections of a fanatic press; without honor or modesty; whose wisdom is paltry cunning, whose valor and manhood have been swallowed up in a corrupt, howling demagogy, and in the marts of dishonest commerce. . . . These [Carolinian] gentlemen are well-bred, courteous and hospitable. A genuine aristocracy, they have time to cultivate their minds, to apply themselves to politics and the guidance of public affairs. They travel and read, love field sports, racing, shooting, hunting, and fishing, are bold horsemen, and good shots. But after all, their state is a modern Sparta – an aristocracy resting on a helotry, and with nothing else to rest upon. . . . Their whole system rests on slavery and as such they defend it. They entertain very exaggerated ideas of the military strength of their community. . . .[7]

The terms "nationalism" and "romantic nationalism" seem to cause endless confusion. Much of the difficulty stems from a tendency to merge the concepts of totally different periods. The net result has been the scrambling of twentieth-century phenomena like Italian fascism and German nazism into a conglomeration with nineteenth-century ideas, until the picture has little in common with historical truth.

The men of the romantic age rarely used the word "nationalist" to describe themselves; and if it is used about them, care must be taken to place the modifier "cultural" in front of it.[8] The nationalism of the romantic thinkers was a cultural nationalism, with the emphasis on "peoples," who were the architects and transmitters of distinct cultures. To these thinkers, "the idea of imposing any nation's ways, speech, or art upon another was repellent." After all, this had been the great rationalist error of the French Revolution on the march, which they felt they were rebelling against. Herder, Wordsworth, Victor Hugo, speaking in the names of German, English, and French romanticisms, all exemplify belief in a nonaggressive, cultural nationalism.[9]

The romantic view did imply longing, striving, and, if necessary, struggling to give expression to repressed cultural nationalism. But this is a far cry from Hitler's legions on the rampage through

7 William Howard Russell, *Pictures of Southern Life* (New York, 1861), pp. 5–8.

8 Jacques Barzun, *Romanticism and the Modern Ego*, p. 128.

9 *Ibid.*, p. 129.

Poland, or the bringing of the blessings of Italian fascism to the barbarians of Athens. There is a dichotomy between Franz Liszt composing Hungarian rhapsodies, in exile from his enslaved fatherland, and the comrades of Horst Wessel singing "Today we own Germany, Tomorrow the whole world."

The confusion in terms becomes all the more understandable, however, in the light of the fact that the land which most conspicuously nurtured the ideas of romantic cultural nationalism was the same land which, in the next century, would pervert those ideas into the vicious tenets of Nazi philosophy. A modern historian has pointed out that nineteenth-century nationalisms in France, England, and Germany were all in the spirit of romantic thinking, but that the French trend was revolutionary democratic, the English aristocratic, and the German a cultural nationalism most closely related to the prevailing romantic concepts. He sees the German movement growing out of the *Sturm und Drang* school of the earlier day, with the concomitant increased interest in "folk language, folk literature, folk customs, and folk personality." These were the precursors of national language, national literature, national culture.[10]

Another present-day scholar, in a brilliant discussion of romanticism, finds that the nationalism of the mid-nineteenth century belongs "in the bulk of its mature conformation primarily to German romanticism."[11] He points to Carlyle and Coleridge as the chief importers and popularizers of these German ideas in England and the United States.[12] It is worth noting that Coleridge, the more restrained of the two, had the greater influence in New England and the North. Carlyle was the favorite in South Carolina and Louisiana.[13] The enlightened humanitarianism of Emerson, Thoreau, Bancroft, and Whitman emerged in the one section of the United States; the idea of Southern nationalism evolved in the other.

Not only Carlyle but Walter Scott, Herder, Michelet, and Lamartine may be identified as "carriers" of European ideas of romantic nationalism to South Carolina.

"Nationalism," according to Hans Kohn, "is first and foremost a state of mind, an act of consciousness, which since the French Revolution has become more and more common to mankind." He goes on to demonstrate that nationalities evolve from the living forces of history and are therefore always fluctuating. Even if a new nationality comes into being, it may perfectly well disappear again, absorbed into a larger or a different nationality. This will happen when the objective bonds that delimit the group are destroyed, for nationality is born of the decision to form a nationality. But the concept, in its developed stage, goes beyond the idea of the group animated by common consciousness. It comprehends also the striving by the group to find expression in the organized activity of a sovereign state. Thus, the nationalism of the nineteenth century was a fusion of an attitude of mind with a particular political form.[14]

[10] Carlton J. H. Hayes and Max H. Boehm, "Nationalism," *Encyclopaedia of the Social Sciences* (15 vols. in 8, New York, 1937), IX, 231–248.

[11] G. Ant. Borgese, "Romanticism," *Encyclopaedia of the Social Sciences,* XIII, 426–433.

[12] *Ibid.*

[13] William E. Dodd, *The Cotton Kingdom,* p. 63.

[14] Hans Kohn, *The Idea of Nationalism* (New York, The Macmillan Company, 1944), pp. 10–20.

The application of these criteria to the history of the rise and fall of the Confederacy, and the subsequent reintegration of the South into the Union, is a documentary implementation of Kohn's definition.

The movement for Southern independence was a manifestation of romantic nationalism, as contrasted with the earlier nonromantic type best exemplified in the creation of the United States of America.[15] This latter type may be conveniently labeled, "the nationalism of the American Revolution"; it had been fed by English national consciousness, evolving since Elizabethan days, transplanted to the new land — and by the natural-rights philosophies of the seventeenth century. American Revolutionary nationalism was a predominantly political occurrence, with the national state formed before, or at least at the same time as, the rising tide of national feeling. The emphasis was on universal standards and values — "inalienable Rights" and "Laws of Nature."

Southern nationalism, on the other hand, stressed the peculiarities of its particular traditions and institutions. In common with the romantic nationalisms of central Europe in the nineteenth century, the frontiers of the existing state and the rising nationality did not coincide. The movement expanded in protest against, and in conflict with, the de facto government. The objective was not to alter the existing political organization, as in the case of the thirteen colonies, but to redraw boundaries that would conform to mythical but credited ethnographic needs.[16] That the realities behind the myth were the institution of Negro slavery and the plantation system do not affect the situation. They merely provide the identifying features.

The evolution of the idea of Southern nationalism, by 1860, was thus in the general stream of mid-nineteenth-century romantic thinking. "The Age of Nationalism," Professor Kohn suggests, "stressed national pasts and traditions against the rationalism of the eighteenth century with its emphasis on the common sense of civilization." The tendency in Europe was to weave the myths of the past and the dreams of the future into the picture of an ideal fatherland — an ideal to be striven for with deep emotional fervor.[17]

This tendency was adapted to the Southern scene. From the past Virginia resurrected her George Washington, who had led an earlier crusade for independence; Maryland recalled her heroes in Randall's stirring stanzas; Carolina cherished the cult of Calhoun; Louisiana pointed to her proud Creole heritage.

All this hewed to the line of romantic nationalism in Europe, where "each new nation looked for its justification to its national heritage — often reinterpreted to suit the supposed needs of the situation — and strove for its glorification."[18]

Romantic nationalism had its influence on the United States as a whole, apart from the specialized phase of the South, during the mid-nineteenth century. The chief manifestation was the "Mission of America" concept — the march toward a trusteeship of liberty and democracy, from which all the world would draw benefit. The romantic historian, Bancroft of Massachusetts, was one of the prophets of this creed.[19]

15 *Ibid.*, pp. 276–293.

16 *Ibid.*, p. 329.

17 Hans Kohn, *Prophets and Peoples — Studies in Nineteenth Century Nationalism* (New York, The Macmillan Company, 1946), pp. 4–9.

18 *Ibid.*

19 Ralph H. Gabriel, *The Course of American Democratic Thought* (New York, The Ronald Press Company, 1940), *passim.*

The maturing of the idea of Southern nationalism in Carolina followed a series of historical events and derived in part from the views of several local personalities. This background was essentially native and nonromantic but, by 1850, possessed a receptivity for the notions of European romantic nationalism. Carlyle, Scott, Herder, Hugo, Michelet, and Lamartine attracted South Carolina readers, who found their ideas congenial.

Carlyle evoked enthusiasm with his argument that the new forces released by the industrial revolution could only be stabilized by an "aristocracy of talent." Scott stimulated Southern nationalism with his mournful recollections of the past glories of a free Scotland. Herder, too, struck a responsive chord with his urging that Germans must cultivate their national genius and look back wistfully at the glamorous days of yore. Victor Hugo typified the climax of the romantic triumph in France; the South cared little for his humanitarian and socialistic ideas but found his patriotic notions appealing. Jules Michelet, romantic historian, emphasized his affection for the folk, in whom the old love of military honor survived, and his contempt for the unchivalrous, commerce-minded, French bourgeoisie. Carolinians could see in this contrast the reflection of themselves and the hated, materialistic Yankees.

Behind the years when Carolinians were discovering encouragement for Southern nationalism, in their favorite European writers, lay a sequence of events which served to put them in a mood receptive to such encouragement. The story properly begins in the late 1820's, when the leadership of the South was moving from the tobacco plantations of the Old Dominion to the intellectual capital of the expanding Cotton Kingdom, at Charleston. The first bow of the new leadership was made in connection with tariff troubles.

South Carolina had opposed the tariff from the earliest days of the republic. The very first Congress, in 1789, had included a group of Carolina representatives known as "anti-tariff men." When the Washington administration sponsored a mild import measure, Senator Pierce Butler of the Palmetto State brought the charge that Congress was oppressing South Carolina and threatened "a dissolution of the Union, with regard to that State, as sure as God was in his firmament." The tariff of 1816, passed in a wave of American national feeling after the War of 1812, found six out of ten Carolina members of the House voting against the bill. John C. Calhoun and the other three who supported the measure were severely censured at home.[20]

Almost the entire South opposed the tariff of 1824. The spreading domain of King Cotton now had a well-defined grievance: the Northeast and the Northwest were uniting to levy taxes on goods exchanged for exported cotton; their protective tariff policy, and concomitant program for internal improvements, was benefiting their entire section at the expense of the South. The policy protected New England mills and furnished funds for linking the seaboard states of the North with the new Northwest by means of canals and turnpikes. The Southern planters paid the bills: they were forced to buy their manufactured supplies in a high market and their chief article of exchange, cotton, had fallen from thirty cents a pound in 1816 to fifteen cents in 1824. In addition, the internal improve-

[20] John G. Van Deusen, *Economic Bases of Disunion in South Carolina* (New York, Columbia University Press, 1928), pp. 17–28.

ments program offered them no compensation; the rivers took their cotton to the shipping points.

When the "Tariff of Abominations" was passed in 1828, all the Southeastern and Southwestern members of the House opposed it, except for three Virginians. In the Senate, only two Southerners supported "the legislative monstrosity."[21]

The opposition to Northern tariff policy was most vociferous in the Palmetto State. From the milieu of this opposition, between 1828 and 1833, several important leaders emerged. They were Thomas Cooper, John C. Calhoun, and the elder Langdon Cheves. Others there were, of course, and the names of many spring to mind — Robert Hayne, A. P. Butler, Chancellor Harper, Francis Pickens, John Lyde Wilson, Joel Poinsett. But the three mentioned were to play especially significant roles in the events that led to the idea of Southern independence; and they began to play those roles in 1828.

Cooper was a gadfly, who buzzed about the ears of people until they listened to his startling suggestions. Calhoun was a vigorous leader, who gave the South group consciousness and his own State a sustained sense of trail-blazing, which it carried right down to the December day in 1860, when it became the first to secede from the Union. Cheves was a cautious and conservative man, who declined to be stampeded but who, once convinced, would give his imagination full play. Cooper was a philosopher with a formula, Calhoun a lawyer with a case, and Cheves a strategist with a plan.

While discussing the attitude of South Carolina toward the hated tariff policy of the 1820's, Channing makes this observation: "Of all the fomenters of discord, Thomas Cooper, an Englishman by birth and then connected with the University of South Carolina, might well be regarded as first in ability and influence." His *Lectures on the Elements of Political Economy* (1826) and other writings of the period receive credit for doing much toward shaping opinion on the tariff. In 1827 he told Senator Martin Van Buren of New York that if the American system were pushed too far, the Carolina legislature would probably recall the State's representatives from Washington.[22]

Cooper's biographer describes him as a disciple of Priestley and Locke, a humanitarian during his early life in England — a Jeffersonian, in the first phase of his American career, when he lived in Pennsylvania — and a man who "came to terms with his new social environment" after he settled in South Carolina in 1820.[23] Seven years after arrival in the Palmetto State, he made the famous declaration that it was time for South Carolina "to calculate the value of the Union." This historic utterance of July 2, 1827, gave rise to shocked expressions of horror, even among some Carolina hotheads, but it had been indelibly burned into the thinking of a generation. It had a habit of cropping out down through the years. Webster and Hayne both alluded to it during their famous debate.[24]

As the second president of South Carolina College, founded in 1805, Thomas Cooper was in a position to inculcate his philosophy and to prepare scores of young men for a dissolution of the Union, which he predicted but did not live to

21 *Ibid.*

22 Channing, *op. cit.*, V, 415–417.

23 Dumas Malone, *The Public Life of Thomas Cooper, 1783–1839* (New Haven, Yale University Press, 1926), *passim.*

24 *Ibid.*, p. 306.

see. Dumas Malone quotes the younger Langdon Cheves, an exponent of Southern nationalism in 1860, as maintaining that the works of Dr. Cooper had done more to determine his political views than had Calhoun, Hayne, or even his illustrious father.[25]

An English traveler, stopping at Columbia, South Carolina, in 1835, had the opportunity to hear Cooper expressing his opinions and to observe the attitude of those who surrounded the strong-minded college president. The visitor received an invitation to dine with Dr. Cooper, several of his professors, and some gentlemen of the Columbia area. After the occasion, he noted in his diary:

> What particularly struck me at this dinner was the total want of caution and reserve in the ultra opinions they expressed about religion and politics; on these topics their conversation was not at all addressed to me but seemed to be the resumption of opinions they were accustomed to express whenever they met and upon all occasions. . . .
>
> I could not help asking, in a good-natured way, if they called themselves Americans yet; the gentleman who had interrupted me before said, "If you ask *me* if I am an American, my answer is *No, Sir,* I am a South Carolinian."
>
> If the children of these Nullifiers are brought up on the same opinions, which they are very likely to be, here are fine elements for future dissension; for imbibing from their infancy the notion that they are born to command, it will be intolerable to them to submit to be, in their own estimation, the drudges of the Northern manufacturers, whom they despise as an inferior race of men. Even now there is nothing a Southern man resents so much as to be called a Yankee. . . .[26]

These significant comments, it should be emphasized, were made twenty-five years before the Civil War. He who made them was a scientist, a Fellow of the Royal Society, a trained observer.

Thomas Cooper's contribution to the idea of Southern independence has been summed up in these words:

> Although he had little to do with the final events of the Nullification controversy, . . . [Cooper's] importance as a pioneer can scarcely be overemphasized. And no man more than he deserves to be termed the schoolmaster of state rights and the prophet of secession.[27]

Cooper was no romantic Southern nationalist as one identifies that type after 1850. The people and the considerations which influenced his philosophy were not in the romantic tradition. Locke and Priestley, utilitarianism and skepticism, were the shaping molds for his thinking. He valued liberty more than union and calculated the worth of the latter purely in terms of its relationship to his adopted State. Yet this hardheaded utilitarian, like the equally hardheaded Calhoun, supplied the basic philosophy which fostered the later romantic concept of Southern nationalism.

John Caldwell Calhoun did more than contribute to the basic philosophy which led to the idea of Southern independence, although he did this with great effectiveness. He thought out the political devices which his section might use to defend itself against an encroaching majority in the councils of the Federal Government. In so doing he stimulated group-consciousness and hoisted the Palmetto flag

[25] *Ibid.*, p. 283.

[26] G. W. Featherstonhaugh, *Excursion through the Slave States,* II, 340–342.

[27] Dumas Malone, "Thomas Cooper and the State Rights Movement in South Carolina, 1823–1830," *The North Carolina Historical Review,* III (April, 1926), 184–197.

of Carolina as the symbol of Southern leadership. "He forged in that busy smithy of his mind," Ralph Gabriel points out, "the intellectual weapons with which the champions of the Cotton Kingdom sought to defeat the democratic principles of majority rule."[28]

In his early years, Calhoun had been an ardent American nationalist. A "War Hawk" who clamored for Britain's scalp in 1812, he had supported the American system in the period immediately following the Peace Treaty of Ghent. In defiance of South Carolina tradition, Congressman Calhoun had voted for the tariff of 1816; he had also advocated internal improvements, especially military roads, and had actually sponsored the bill which chartered the second Bank of the United States.

It was the passage of the "Tariff of Abominations," in 1828, which brought him forward in a quite different role. The former American nationalist now became the exponent of the thesis that a state could refuse obedience to an act of Congress and at the same time not be involved in rebellion. Channing attributes the sudden turnabout principally to Calhoun's ambitions for the presidency and the need for the support of his own nullification-minded State.[29] The motives behind his grasping the torch of sectional leadership, in 1828, are of less concern to present purposes than the fact that he did so.

In a letter written May 1, 1833, President Jackson expressed the conviction that the tariff had been only the pretext for crystallizing nullification sentiment in South Carolina. The real objective of the agitators, he insisted, was not tariff reform but the establishment of a Southern confederacy. "The next pretext," he suggested, "will be the negro, or slavery, questions." The other cotton states, however, had shown slight sympathy for Carolina's bold stand between 1828 and 1833 – and the tobacco states to the north were conspicuously indifferent.[30] The nullification episode was a South Carolina, not a sectional, incident; but it would have far-reaching implications for the entire Southland as the years went on. It prepared the minds of men for disunion.

As for Calhoun's place in the march toward Southern nationalism, he was "the chosen leader of a predetermined course, in no sense a driver." South Carolina was intent on courses both in 1832, and again in 1850, which Calhoun did not originate but to which he gave his powerful support. With matchless clarity he propounded the point of view of his State, leading the rest of the Cotton Kingdom closer and closer to the time when it would adopt the Carolina course for its own. Yet all the while he preached a certain moderation, holding his associates back from too precipitate action, hoping always for solution within the framework of Union.[31]

Speaking in Charleston in August, 1848, Calhoun still persisted in the belief that a Southern party would enable the South to achieve her ends in cooperation with sympathizers in the North. But he admitted that if this procedure failed to check the aggressive spirit of the abolitionists, then armed resistance by a united South would be indicated. "Though the union is dear to us, our honor and our liberty are dearer."[32]

[28] Gabriel, *op. cit.*, p. 103.

[29] Channing, *op. cit.*, V, 419–432.

[30] *Ibid.*, V, 427.

[31] David Duncan Wallace, *The History of South Carolina,* III, 123–124.

[32] Philip May Hamer, *The Secession Movement in South Carolina, 1847–1852* (Allentown, Pa., H. R. Haas and Company, 1918), pp. 22–23.

Ulrich Phillips felt that, "as long as Calhoun lived, his mighty championship exerted a subduing influence upon Southerners in private life." The Carolina statesman was ever reluctant to believe the impending conflict irrepressible. In his last years he seemed to waver between the hope of solution within the frame of the Union and the fear that Southern secession would become necessary. Many of his adherents wavered with him. Even after his death on the last day of March, 1850, Calhoun's project for a convention at Nashville triumphed over the call of the hotheads for an open break with the North, as proper answer to Clay's compromise measures.[33]

Such was Calhoun in life. Death made him a symbol for Southern nationalism. During the decade between 1850 and the Civil War, he emerges from the pages of the *Southern Quarterly Review* as the romantic leader of the crusade for Southern independence.

As early as November, 1850, appeared the lengthy comment by "S.D.M. of Tuscaloosa, Alabama," occasioned by the obituary speeches honoring Calhoun in the United States Senate.[34] That comment was characteristic of many others to follow.

> One thing is certain, that, in this crisis of affairs, the bulwark of our strength is gone. We shall no more see the proud crest in the field of battle in defense of us and ours. . . . His mantle will yet fall upon worthy shoulders. We are still in possession of his chart and compass. . . . All over that chart you will see the beacon lights of liberty pointing out the way that leads to a people's glory and renown, and showing in what way only we may avoid that which leads to a people's shame.

Some months later, when the shadows of the impending struggle were growing even darker, the *Quarterly* seized the instance of the appearance in print of Hammond's "Oration on Calhoun" to glorify further the Carolinian statesman as a symbol of Southern nationalism. In this article, Calhoun's former "erroneous" support of the American system is attributed to "wide patriotism"; and his later leadership of the South, when he "very properly reversed his views," is treated as a normal development of greatness.[35]

The cult of Calhoun as a symbol of Southern nationalism – which grew up after his death – was completely in the romantic tradition. It is reminiscent of the manner in which the Young France group, under the guidance of Hector Berlioz, had seized upon the recently deceased Beethoven and glorified him as the symbol of romantic music.[36] Just as Berlioz, Hugo, Lamartine, and the adherents of Saint-Simon imbued the figure of the composer with their own artistic and social ideals, so did the Southern nationalists of Carolina endow the figure of John C. Calhoun with the regalia of positive leadership in the movement for Southern independence. Calhoun, as a symbol after death, became almost as important in that movement as Calhoun, the defender of Southern rights within the framework of the Union, had been in his lifetime.

In addition to Calhoun and Cooper, Langdon Cheves made significant contributions to the growth of the idea of

[33] Phillips, *op. cit.*, p. 38.

[34] *Southern Quarterly Review*, XVIII (November, 1850), 486–509.

[35] *Ibid.*, XX (July, 1851), 107–117.

[36] Leo Schrade, *Beethoven in France – The Growth of an Idea* (New Haven, Yale University Press, 1942), pp. 39–108.

Southern nationalism. Cheves had formulated a plan for solving Carolina's problems as far back as the nullification controversy of 1828.

The wisdom of adopting a nullification program had divided South Carolina into two well-defined factions. Those who favored the program were led by Calhoun, Dr. Cooper, Robert Hayne, Francis Pickens, R. B. Rhett, and John Lyde Wilson. Opposed to nullification were the Union men – Senator William Smith, William Drayton, Joel R. Poinsett, James Louis Petigru, and other respected individuals.[37]

The leaders of the Unionist faction did not underestimate the personal prestige or the long-pull ambitions of the Nullifiers. On the other hand, they seemed to feel that the rank and file of the people were adverse to drastic action, in 1833. During April that year one Unionist wrote to another:

What have you been doing this great while? On the plantation, I suppose. Do you hear much from the Revolutioners lately? I believe they intend to open *for a Southern Confederacy* soon. . . . But they will not commit themselves just now. The people, I fair think, are settling down to a more composed and moderate tone. They are not so much inflamed about politics, it seems to me, and more inclined to mind their own business. These are good symptoms, so far; they may be delusive, however. . . . We who have got the chivalry against us must carefully cultivate the good will of our neighbors. Adieu.[38]

The reference in this letter to possible sentiment in favor of a Southern confederacy, among the Nullifiers, brings to mind the positive plan advocated by Langdon Cheves.

Cheves had remained aloof from both parties. He manifested little love for the Union but condemned nullification by a single state as an impractical procedure. To his mind, the problem of the tariff went far beyond the borders of South Carolina. The entire South would suffer from its blighting effects. Therefore, the entire South should act together. He proposed that representatives of all the Southern states should gather for a convention and that the convention should deliver an ultimatum to the Congress in Washington: either abandon the protecting policy or take the responsibility for the formation of a Southern confederacy.[39]

Thus, three points of view appeared in the struggle over the tariff between 1828 and 1833 – cooperation with the Union at all costs, nullification of "unfair" Federal laws by South Carolina alone, and action by a united Southland. Clay's compromise tariff bill terminated the exciting episode and the antipathies of the three factions were temporarily forgotten.

But fourteen years later, when David Wilmot introduced in Congress his famous proviso prohibiting slavery in any territory that might be acquired incidental to the Mexican war, memories returned to the thoughts expressed by the Carolina leaders of 1832. Calhoun led the fight to beat the Wilmot Proviso in the Senate but the fat was in the fire and once again feelings ran high in the Palmetto State. This time the tension was

[37] Van Deusen, *op. cit.*, pp. 46–49.

[38] James Louis Petigru to William Elliott, dated "Charleston, 14 April 1833." Included in James Petigru Carson, ed., *Life, Letters and Speeches of James Louis Petigru* (Washington, D. C., W. H. Lowdermilk and Company, 1920), p. 122. Italics mine.

[39] Van Deusen, *op. cit.*, pp. 46–49.

not limited to South Carolina alone; the whole country was aroused. State legislatures "above the Line" passed resolutions extolling Congressman Wilmot. In the Southland, people looked toward Carolina, to watch for the formulation of a policy.

Between 1847 and 1852, three parties sprang to activity in the Palmetto State. Their programs recall the earlier alignments in the nullification incident. The three groups were known as: Immediate Secessionists, Unionists, Cooperationists. The Secessionists, led by R. B. Rhett, Governor Seabrook, Maxcy Gregg, and Francis Pickens advocated immediate withdrawal by South Carolina from the United States. The Unionist party, headed by Joel Poinsett, James L. Petigru, William Grayson, and Benjamin Perry of Greenville stood for "Southern rights within the Union."[40]

The party which merits particular attention, for it was the faction that eventually carried the day, bore the confusing label, "Cooperationists." This was the real Southern nationalist group. Its leaders included Langdon Cheves, the man with a plan back in 1832, Senators Barnwell and A. P. Butler, and Memminger, Hammond, Orr, and others. The Cooperationists were resolved that South Carolina should not find herself isolated again as she had in Nullification days. This time she must go forward with the support of the rest of the South. The aggressive North was not threatening the life of the Palmetto State alone. It was a whole "homogeneous section" that was under attack. If South Carolina is to lead the resistance, then it must only be with the *cooperation* of her Southern sisters. If the latter are not yet ready to recognize the necessity of separate nationality, then Carolina must wait until they are ready — striving meanwhile to guide them down the road toward independence.[41]

The Cooperationists made their views known during the election year 1848, when, operating out of Charleston, they attempted to get the Democratic party of the State to endorse an all-Southern presidential ticket of Taylor and A. P. Butler in opposition to Lewis Cass. They were beaten when the legislature voted for presidential electors, but their move stimulated the idea of an increasingly self-conscious Southern bloc.[42]

The Unionist faction, during this period, was the weakest of the three, the struggle for power in the State quickly narrowing down to the Cooperationists and the Immediate Secessionists. The latter party drew its main support from the interior sections and revolved about the central figure of R. B. Rhett. A rather inflexible individual, Rhett "saw later issues always from the standpoint of 1832." On the other hand, the Cooperationists, drawing their strength from Charleston and its intellectual, social, and financial dependencies, boasted no single, dominating personality. Langdon Cheves, who had been the first of the leaders to espouse the idea of Southern nationalism, was important; but so also were Andrew Pickens Butler and R. W. Barnwell. Those three probably wielded the principal power in the group.[43]

A head-on collision between the two chief factions in South Carolina political life was averted in 1850. Calhoun, adopting a course different from either but closer to the nationalists' than to Rhett's,

40 Wallace, *op. cit.*, III, 119–132.

41 *Ibid.*

42 Nathaniel W. Stephenson, "Southern Nationalism in South Carolina, in 1851," *American Historical Review,* XXXVI (January, 1931), 314–335.

43 *Ibid.*

strove to consolidate the South as a unit within the framework of the Union. To this end he gave his ebbing strength, in the early months of 1850. The result was the Nashville Convention, held in November of that year after the great statesman had already died.[44] And at the Nashville Convention Langdon Cheves made his powerful bid for "united secession for the slave-holding states" and painted the picture of "one of the most splendid empires on which the sun ever shone."[45]

Outside of Cheves's speech, the Nashville Convention was lifeless and dull. The passage of Clay's compromise measures had produced a temporary calm in the political arena. But when the Carolinian nationalist delegates returned to Charleston, they were imbued with implemented confidence in their cause. Early in 1851 they instituted a propaganda campaign against immediate secession of the Palmetto State – for which Rhett continued to agitate – and in behalf of eventual formation of a Southern confederacy. The Charleston *Mercury* was spokesman for the fire-eating Rhett, while the Cooperationists launched their attack in pamphlets, spread not only through South Carolina but all over the Cotton Kingdom.[46]

In the election of delegates to a Southern convention during the fall of 1851, a test plebiscite between the two parties took place. The Rhett faction was soundly beaten, attributing its defeat to the "controlling interests of trade" centered at Charleston and dominated by Barnwell, Butler, and Cheves.[47]

The South Carolinians split in 1851, not over the question of giving the Union another trial – which was the case in Georgia during this period – but over a much more subtle issue: the issue of secession by a single state versus the emerging recognition that the South had become a single community and must act as such.[48] The idea which prevailed in South Carolina in 1851 was the idea which would prevail through the entire Southland ten years later. That idea was Southern nationalism – a product basically of independent native growth but with a coloring of European romantic notions.

Samuel Phillips Day, an English visitor who talked with many leaders of Southern thought in 1861, sensed the significance of that romantic nationalism. He wrote in his diary:

> This is no civil strife: no struggle of Guelph and Ghibelline; no contest between York and Lancaster; but a war of alien races, distinct nationalities, and antagonistic governments. Cavalier and Roundhead no longer designate parties, but nations, whose separate foundations . . . were laid on Plymouth Rock and the banks of the James River. Whoever would rightly understand the causes of the present convulsion in America must find their explanation in the irreconcilable character of the Cavalier and Puritan, the antagonisms of agricultural and commercial communities, and the conflicts between free and slave labor, when the manufacturing and navigating interests attempt to wrest the sceptre from agriculture by unfriendly legislation.[49]

The failure of Rhett and his Immediate Secessionist party left South Carolina, in 1852, within the Union but with an eye to a future break. For the next eight years her Southern nationalist leaders

44 *Ibid.*

45 See notes 3, 4, and 5 of this chapter.

46 Stephenson, *op. cit.*, pp. 314–335.

47 *Ibid.*

48 *Ibid.*

49 Samuel Phillips Day, *Down South – Or an Englishman's Experience at the Seat of the American War*, I, 208.

would be working toward the day when the rest of the Cotton Kingdom would be ready to act.[50] The election of Lincoln in November, 1860, heralded the arrival of der Tag.

Between 1852 and 1860 the Southern nationalists controlled the politics of the Palmetto State. Powerful supporters gathered around the standard of Cheves and Butler and Robert Barnwell. When the first of two of these veteran leaders died in 1857, capable successors stepped into their places. The new leadership included Congressman James Orr, C. G. Memminger, James Chesnut, Jr., and the influential writers, Simms and Timrod. Gravitating toward the Cooperationists, also, was D. F. Jamison, lawyer, planter, politician, and historian. Jamison had toyed with the idea of separate action by South Carolina, in 1851; but his growing enthusiasm for Southern nationalism brought him into the camp of the Co-operationists.

The agitators for a future confederacy did not limit themselves to the local politics of their own State. Having seized control of the propaganda machine, *The Southern Rights Association,* they proceeded to flood the Cotton Kingdom with pamphlets. This association had originally been founded by Maxcy Gregg and R. B. Rhett, the secessionist firebrands, for their own purposes. The Cooperationists took the material, already prepared, which served their particular purposes, added more, and distributed the leaflets all over Dixie.[51]

One such pamphlet, first published in 1850, was *The Rightful Remedy* by Edward B. Bryan. In it, "the slaveholders of the South particularly, and the citizens of the slaveholding states" are exhorted to unite in order to defend "the most time-honored institution extant," and to set up their own government.[52]

A similar treatise, sponsored by the Carolinian Southern nationalists, declared that the establishment of a separate confederacy "with a homogeneous population and an united government" would relieve the South from her false and dangerous situation of being a nation within a nation.[53]

Simms, in his *Southern Quarterly Review,* gave preferred position to such articles as "Is Southern Civilization Worth Preserving?"[54] This lengthy appeal for Southern nationalism, in 1851, set the tone for many others which followed during the next ten years.

Impartial observers had no trouble in recognizing the role of South Carolina in the crusade. The correspondent of the London *Times* described the Palmetto State, in May, 1861, as having been "the *fons et origo* of the secession doctrines and their development into the full life of the Confederate States."[55]

The official historian of the State of South Carolina has characterized the period between 1852 and 1860, in the State's history, as "Waiting for the South." Discussing the dominant mood of that eight-year stretch, he asserted:

> Here again we have that ideal of Southern nationalism voicing the feeling that the South was organically one, despite the constant insistence as a matter of legal theory on the sovereignty of the individual state. The latter

[50] Hamer, *op. cit.*, Preface.

[51] *Ibid.*, pp. 56–143.

[52] Edward B. Bryan, *The Rightful Remedy* (Charleston, S. C., 1850), *passim.*

[53] William H. Trescot, *The Position and Course of the South* (Charleston, S. C., 1850), pp. 6–18.

[54] *Southern Quarterly Review,* XIX (January, 1851), 189–225.

[55] William H. Russell, *op. cit.*, p. 24.

was mainly defensive tactics against a hostile North.[56]

The election of Lincoln liberated South Carolina from her self-imposed restraint. She knew now that the years of waiting were over – that where she would lead, others would follow. The ideal of Southern nationalism could become the actuality of a Southern nation. Judge J. S. Black of Pennsylvania, Buchanan's attorney general, put his finger on the true role of the Palmetto State. "Like Athens," he wrote of Carolina, "you control Greece – you have made and you will control, this revolution by your indomitable spirit."[57]

As soon as it was clear that the United States had elected a president committed to an anti-slavery platform, the South Carolina legislature voted to call a State convention. The delegates met at Columbia on December 17, 1860, fully conscious that they were about to sign an ordinance of secession. Because of a case of smallpox in the town, they adjourned to Charleston on the eighteenth. Two days later, they voted unanimously to take their State out of the Union.[58]

The proceedings of the convention are significant, for they indicate that the delegates were thinking in far bigger terms than the secession of South Carolina. A careful perusal of the *Journal of the Convention of the People of South Carolina* reveals exactly what they had in mind.

From such perusal one fact stands out immediately. The Southern nationalist faction was in complete control of the gathering. A. P. Butler and Langdon Cheves had died three years before but Langdon Cheves, Jr., was on hand to represent his father's point of view. Senator Robert Barnwell, last of the old triumvirate, was very much in evidence. D. F. Jamison was elected temporary chairman and, a few hours later, permanent president of the convention. He was elected on the fourth ballot, triumphing over two other Southern nationalists, Orr and Chesnut.[59]

When Jamison was made temporary chairman at the beginning of the convention, in Columbia, he addressed the assemblage with these words:

> Written Constitutions are worthless unless they are written at the same time in the hearts, and founded on the interests of a people; and there is no common bond of sympathy between the North and the South. All efforts to preserve this Union will not only be fruitless, but fatal to the less numerous section. . . .
>
> At the moment of inaugurating a great movement like the present, I trust that we will go forward and not be diverted from our purpose by influences from without. In the outset of this movement, I can offer you no better motto than Danton's, at the commencement of the French Revolution: "To dare! and again to dare! and without end to dare!"[60]

These are clearly the ideas of a man thinking in larger terms than the secession of a single state. Furthermore, Jamison's allusion to Danton's romantic oratory arouses suspicion that this Southern nationalist may have had some

[56] Wallace, *op. cit.,* III, 133–150.

[57] Gaillard Hunt, ed., "Narrative and Letter of William Henry Trescot, Concerning the Negotiations between South Carolina and President Buchanan, in December, 1860," *American Historical Review,* XIII (April, 1908), 549.

[58] Wallace, *op. cit.,* III, 153–156.

[59] *Journal of the Convention of the People of South Carolina, Held in 1860–61* (Charleston, 1861), pp. 8–10. Hereafter cited as *Convention Journal.*

[60] *Ibid.,* pp. 3–5.

knowledge of the notions of nationalism associated with the European romantic movements.

David Flavel Jamison had been a student at South Carolina College in the days of Thomas Cooper, and Langdon Cheves, Jr., gave more credit for shaping his political views to Cooper than to his illustrious father. Jamison practiced law for two years, then turned planter. From 1836 to 1848 he represented his district of Orangeburg in the South Carolina legislature, where he sponsored the bill for establishing the South Carolina Military Academy. He attended the Nashville Convention with the elder Cheves, in 1850; and later played with the idea of separate action by South Carolina, during the excitement of 1851. In the years that followed he found his philosophies best expressed by the Southern nationalist group and became part of the circle surrounding William Gilmore Simms. At the secession convention, he represented Simms's district of Barnwell and was, in a sense, the mouthpiece of the romantic Southern nationalists associated with Simms and Timrod.[61]

Jamison's chief interest in life was historical studies. His biographer says:

> In the *Southern Quarterly Review* for January and July, 1843, January, April, and October, 1844, and October, 1849, there were reviews of Guizot, Mignet, Herder, Michelet, and Lamartine, which either by signature or internal evidence are to be ascribed to him. . . . To the Southern planter the lessons of modern European history seemed plain, and it was doubtless these studies as much as the long controversy over the Wilmot Proviso that matured his political philosophy.[62]

The cat is out of the bag. This man Jamison, presiding officer at the South Carolina secession convention, was not only the product of the many native influences which promoted the idea of Southern nationalism in the Palmetto State. He was, also, steeped in the ideas of romantic nationalism coming out of the continent of Europe. His political philosophy, shaped by Cooper and the procession of local events, had been matured by Herder, Michelet, and Lamartine.

Jamison's commentary on Herder's *Outline of a Philosophy of the History of Man* was a lengthy, scholarly affair, which appeared as the first article in an 1844 issue of the *Southern Quarterly Review*.[63] The analysis of Herder's masterpiece was clear and thorough. Jamison was anxious not only to understand the implications of cultural nationalism but to have others understand them also.

The digression from the South Carolina secession convention has revealed the sort of man who presided over its deliberations. That man seems the very symbol of the growth of the idea of Southern nationalism in his State—embodying an experience with the chief native influences behind the idea and a familiarity with the notions of romantic nationalism, coming out of the lands across the sea.

What of the secession convention itself? Did the delegates think that they were voting merely for dissolving the bonds of union between their State and the others?

The *Journal* of the convention makes it perfectly clear that the men present were confident that they were launching a movement for a Southern confederacy. When the first meeting took place, com-

61 Robert L. Meriwether, "David Flavel Jamison," *Dictionary of American Biography*, IX, 604–605.

62 *Ibid.*

63 *Southern Quarterly Review*, V (April, 1844), 265–311.

missioners from Alabama and Mississippi, appointed by their respective governors, joined the group. Letters of encouragement arrived from the states of Florida and Arkansas. Georgia offered volunteers in case South Carolina's action should lead to armed reprisals.[64]

The day after the convention had moved to Charleston, President Jamison announced that Commissioner Elmore of Alabama had handed him a telegram from Governor A. B. Moore of that State, which read, "Tell the Convention to listen to no propositions of compromise or delay." A few hours later the delegates voted to send representatives to all slaveholding states, inviting them to join South Carolina in a new confederacy.[65] The next day, December 20, the convention passed the ordinance of secession. The sequence of events, the importance given to the communications sent by the other slaveholding states, the language of the delegates, all indicate that the idea of Southern nationalism was paramount.

If this is not enough, the formal action taken by the convention completes the evidence. The chief business on December 26 was the passage of an ordinance "Recommending and Providing for a Convention of the Slaveholding States of the United States, to form the Constitution of a Southern Confederacy." The meeting at Montgomery, Alabama, in February, 1861, was the direct result of this resolution.[66]

One of the most interesting developments of the convention was the emergence of R. B. Rhett, the old leader of the Immediate Secessionist faction, as an exponent of Southern nationalism. When he moved for a committee to prepare an address to the people of the Southern states, he was made chairman of such a committee. His "Address to the Slaveholding States" portrayed the South as a distinct civilization, in the best romantic-nationalist manner. He went so far as to declare that the Federal Constitution had been an experiment from the first, an attempt to unite two peoples of different character and different institutions and that the experiment had failed.[67] The interests of the two old hostile factions — the Immediate Secessionists and the Cooperationists — came together in the convention of December, 1860. Robert Rhett was now eager to preach the doctrines of the romantic nationalists.

The chips were down at the South Carolina secession convention. People recognized that most of the former talk about State rights had been window dressing. It was Southern rights that they were thinking about. An Alabama representative, present in official capacity, told the delegates:

> Information obtained on diligent inquiry, in the last few days, justifies me in saying that the gallant sons of North Carolina and Virginia are now ready to rally around the standard of *Southern Rights and Honor*, which you have so gloriously raised. . . . To the bold, deliberate, and decisive action of your body are the people of the South indebted for the great movement which must end in the vindication of their rights.[68]

That most astute of all Southern historians, Ulrich Phillips, maintained that

64 *Convention Journal, passim.*

65 *Ibid.*, pp. 28–35.

66 *Ibid.*, pp. 99–100.

67 Laura A. White, *Robert Barnwell Rhett: Father of Secession* (New York, The Century Company, 1937), pp. 188–190; *Convention Journal, passim.*

68 *Convention Journal,* p. 2121. Italics mine.

State rights formed no object of devotion among the antebellum leaders for their own sake but only as a means of securing Southern rights. "State sovereignty," he pithily explained, "was used to give the insignia of legality to a stroke for national independence."[69]

Regarding the fact that the framers of the Confederate Constitution gave official sanction to the State rights principle, Phillips concluded that this was, in large part, a mere saving of face. He said, "The movement was not so much a flying from the old center as a flying to the new; and it was not by chance that Timrod wrote in 1861, 'at last we are a nation among nations,' and entitled his poem of celebration 'Ethnogenesis.'"[70]

Phillips' allusion to the poem "Ethnogenesis" is a happy one. He felt that "it was not by chance" that Timrod wrote in the vein that he did, with the emphasis on Southern nationalism. Nor was it by chance, either – it should be added – that he who wrote in this vein and who called his poem "Ethnogenesis" was a South Carolina romantic poet. In Henry Timrod's State, and among Henry Timrod's friends, the idea of Southern nationalism had matured. Who better could hail the meeting of the first Southern Congress, at Montgomery, with these lines?

Hath not the morning dawned with added
  light?
And shall not evening call another star
Out of the infinite regions of the night,
To mark this day in heaven? At last we are
A nation among nations; and the world
Shall soon behold in many a distant port
  Another flag unfurled![71]

69 Phillips, *op. cit.*, pp. 59–60.

70 *Ibid.*

71 Henry Timrod, "Ethnogenesis," *Poems of Henry Timrod*, pp. 150–154.

J. G. Randall: A BLUNDERING GENERATION

WHEN one visits a moving picture, or reads Hergesheimer's *Swords and Roses*, which is much the same thing, he may gather the impression that the Civil War, fought in the days before mechanized divisions, bombs, and tanks, was a kind of *chanson de geste* in real life. "The Civil War in America," writes Hergesheimer, "was the last of all wars fought in the grand manner. It was the last romantic war, when army corps fought as individuals and lines of assault . . . charged the visible enemy." "The war created a heroism . . . that clad fact in the splendor of battle flags."[1]

Hergesheimer feeds his readers chunks of sombre beauty, winterless climate, air stirred with faint cool music, fine houses, Spanish moss and cypress, trumpet vine and bay blossom, live oak and linden, bridal wreath, japonica, moonflower, and honeysuckle. In his foreword to "Dear Blanche" he writes: "Here is a book of swords . . . of old-fashioned dark roses . . . [of] the simpler loveliness of the past." His pages live up to the foreword. He gives dear Blanche "The Rose of Mississippi," "The Lonely Star," "Shadows on the Sea," and "Gold Spurs." Of "Jeb" Stuart he says:

> Ladies in Maryland gave him the spurs and ladies wherever he chanced to be gave him rosebuds. . . . Naturally he was in the cavalry. He was different. . . . [He] wore a brown felt hat . . . with . . . sweeping black plume; . . . his boots in action were heavy, . . . afterwards he changed them for immaculate boots of patent leather worked with gold thread; but he danced as well as fought in his spurs.[2]

Colorful touches fill in the picture: red-lined cape, French sabre, yellow sash and tassels, The Bugles Sang Truce, The Dew is on the Blossom, orders given when asleep, animal vitality dancing in brilliant eyes.

Escapists may put what they will between the covers of a book; unfortunately the historian must be a realist. Whatever may be the thrill, or the emotional spree, of treating the Civil War romantically, it may be assumed that this has not been neglected. A different task, therefore, will be attempted in these pages – that of weighing a few Civil War realities, examining some of the irrational ideas of war "causation," and pondering some aspects of the Civil War mind.[3]

Without stressing the obvious fact that recent examples of heroism have matched any Civil War exploit, or that aviation is

[1] Joseph Hergesheimer, *Swords and Roses*, 297, 299.

[2] *Ibid.*, 267.

[3] Howard K. Beale's "What Historians Have Said about the Causes of the Civil War" (*Theory and Practice in Historical Study: A Report of the Committee on Historiography* [Social Science Research Council *Bulletin* No. 54], 55–102) is unequaled for scholarly coverage of this complex subject and for compression of elaborate research in brief form.

as smart as cavalry, it is sufficient to note a few comparisons. If World War I produced more deaths, the Civil War produced more American deaths. If weapons have become more brutal, at least medicine and sanitation have advanced. One seldom reads of the Civil War in terms of sick and wounded. Medical officers of the sixties repeated the experience of a British medical officer in the Burmese War who advised his commander how to avoid scurvy and was told: "Medical opinions are very good when called for."[4] A Union surgeon at Bull Run reported extreme difficulty in inducing field officers to listen to complaints of disease resulting from foul tents into which fresh air was "seldom if ever" admitted.[5] Because ambulances were on the wrong side of the road, this also at Bull Run, twelve thousand troops had to pass before some of the wounded could be taken to the emergency hospital.[6] Wounded men arriving from the field were thrust into freight cars where they lay on the bare floor without food for a day; numbers died on the road.[7] One of the officers refused hospital admittance to wounded soldiers not of his regiment.[8] Medical supplies were thrown away for want of transportation,[9] injured men were exposed to heavy rain,[10] gangrene resulted from minor wounds.[11]

Romance and glory suggest at least the memory of a name. This implies an identified grave, but after making calculations based upon the official medical history issued by the surgeon general, the student would have to inform dear Blanche, or perhaps Mr. Ripley, that if the surgeon general's figures are right the unknown dead for the Civil War exceeded the number killed in battle! In round numbers there were about 110,000 Union deaths from battle, while the surgeon general reported that in November 1870 there were 315,555 soldier graves, of which only 172,109 had been identified by name,[12] leaving over 143,000 unidentified graves. The number of Union soldiers known in the adjutant general's records to have died during the war is much greater than the number identified as to burial or reburial. It must be remembered that the soldier regularly carried no means of identification, that graves of men buried by comrades were marked by hasty devices, that Confederates appropriated Union arms and clothing, that teamsters, refugees, camp followers, or even fugitive slaves might have been buried with soldiers, and that the number reported as killed in action, this being less than half the deaths, was inaccurate.[13] A full examination of these and other factors would throw further light on the matter; yet after making all such allowances, the vast number of the nameless leaves the inquiring mind unsatisfied. It is no more satisfactory to realize that about half the Union army became human waste in one form or another, as dead, disabled, deserting, or imprisoned.[14]

[4] Joseph K. Barnes, ed., *The Medical and Surgical History of the War of the Rebellion* (Washington, second issue, 1875), Pt. 1, Vol. I, Append., 2.

[5] *Ibid.*, Append., 1.

[6] *Ibid.*, Append., 2.

[7] *Ibid.*, Append., 7.

[8] *Ibid.*, Append., 3.

[9] *Ibid.*, Append., 99.

[10] *Ibid.*, Append., 146.

[11] *Ibid.*, Append., 137.

[12] *Ibid.*, Intro., xxxiii.

[13] *Ibid.*, Intro., xxxiii, xxxiv, xxxvi; Charles G. Souder, Medical Corps, U. S. Army, to the author, November 17, 1939.

[14] Of 360,000 Union deaths (round numbers), 110,000 resulted from battle, over 224,500 from disease, and nearly 25,000 from miscellaneous causes including suicide. United States Adjutant

"Jeb" Stuart may have worn gold spurs, but the common soldier was more familiar with vermin. Sashes may have adorned generals, but privates were often in rags. It was reported that one of the army surgeons boarded for an entire winter on Sanitary Commission stores.[15] Camps were dirty, sanitation was faulty, cooking was shiftless. Reporting on one of the hospitals, an inspector referred to a leaky roof, broken glass, dirty stairs, insufficient sanitary facilities, and unclean disgusting beds.[16] The soldier who was brutally struck by a sentry of his own company or who contracted malaria would hardly think of his experience as a thing of romance. Without exposing all the euphemisms that obscure the truth of this subject, it may be noted that the great majority of Union deaths were from causes medically regarded as preventable, leaving aside the cynical assumption that war itself is not preventable.

Pneumonia, typhus, cholera, miasmic fever, and the like hardly find their way into the pages of war romance, but they wrought more havoc than bayonets and guns. Where there was danger of infection the rule-of-thumb principle of the Civil War surgeon was to amputate,[17] and from operating tables, such as they were, at Gettysburg, arms and legs were carried away in wagon loads. Discipline was slack, desertion was rampant, corruption was rife. Individual injustices of the war were shocking. Some generals got credit that was undeserved, others were broken by false report or slandered by an investigating committee of Congress. The men who languished in prison were several times more numerous than those killed by bullets. That there was heroism in the war is well known, but to thousands the war was as romantic as prison rats and as gallant as typhoid or syphilis.

2

One does not often speak or read of the war in reality, of its blood and filth, of mutilated flesh, and other revolting things.[18] This restraint is necessary, but it ought to be recognized that the war is not presented when one writes of debates in Congress, of flanking movements, of

General's letter to the author, November 3, 1939. Suicides are mentioned by J. J. Woodward who wrote the introduction to Barnes, *Medical and Surgical History*, Pt. 1, Vol. I, xxxvii. Woodward also (intro., xlii) states that there were 285,545 men discharged from the Union army for disability. The adjutant general mentions 223,535 discharged for "physical disability" (letter to author, November 3, 1939). Union soldiers who became prisoners numbered nearly 195,000; Union deserters, not counting draft dodgers, may be conservatively estimated at about 200,000. J. G. Randall, *Civil War and Reconstruction*, 432, 439; Fred A. Shannon, *Organization and Administration of the Union Army, 1861–1865*, II, 179 n. It thus appears that approximately a million were among the dead, disabled, deserting, or imprisoned. A careful statistician has stated: "It is doubtful if there were 2,000,000 individuals actually in [Union] service during the [Civil] war." William F. Fox, *Regimental Losses in the American Civil War, 1861–65*, 527.

15 Lewis H. Steiner, "Account of the Field Relief Corps of the U. S. Sanitary Commission of the Army of the Potomac," *Sanitary Commission, Pamphlet No. 72* (New York, 1863), 6.

16 H. W. Bellows, "Notes of a Preliminary Sanitary Survey of the Forces of the United States in the Ohio and Mississippi Valleys near Midsummer, 1861," *Sanitary Commission, Pamphlet No. 26* (Washington, 1861), 15.

17 "In army practice, attempts to save a limb which might be perfectly successful in civil life, cannot be made . . . . Conservative surgery is here an error; in order to save life, the limb must be sacrificed." Frederick L. Olmsted, "Report of a Committee of the Medical Members of the Sanitary Commission on the Subject of Amputations," *Sanitary Commission F* (Washington, 1861), 5.

18 In postwar reminiscence the Union soldier might hold forth on the subject of the war as a purifying force and a builder of character where the same individual during the war recorded his feeling of disgust with what was around him, of degradation, and of the tearing down of character.

retreats and advances, of cavalry and infantry, of divisions doing this and brigades doing that. In the sense of full realism war cannot be discussed. The human mind will not stand for it. For the very word "war" the realist would have to substitute some such term as "organized murder" or "human slaughterhouse." In drama as distinguished from melodrama murder often occurs offstage. In most historical accounts, especially military narratives, the war is offstage in that its stench and hideousness do not appear.

In a subject so vast, yet often so imperfectly treated, it is difficult to achieve a full realization of how Lincoln's generation stumbled into a ghastly war, how it blundered during four years of indecisive slaughter, and how the triumph of the Union was spoiled by the manner in which the victory was used. In the hateful results of the war over long decades one finds partisanship at its worst. To see the period as it was is to witness uninspired spectacles of prejudice, error, intolerance, and selfish grasping. The Union army was inefficiently raised, poorly administered, and often badly commanded. In government there was deadlock, cross purpose, and extravagance. One can say that Lincoln was honest, but not that the country was free from corruption during the Lincoln administration. There was cotton plundering, army-contract graft, and speculative greed. Where Lincoln was at his best, where he was moderate, temperate, and far-seeing, he did not carry his party with him. Even those matters dissociated from the war, such as homesteading and railroad extension, came to be marred by exploitation and crooked finance. The period of the Civil War and the tawdry era of Jim Fisk and Jay Gould were one and the same generation.

If it was a "needless war," a "repressible conflict," then indeed was the generation misled in its unctuous fury. To suppose that the Union could not have been continued or slavery outmoded without the war and without the corrupt concomitants of the war, is hardly an enlightened assumption. If one questions the term "blundering generation," let him inquire how many measures of the time he would wish copied or repeated if the period were to be approached with a clean slate and to be lived again. Most of the measures are significant as things to be avoided. Of course it is not suggested that the generation of the sixties had any copyright on blundering.

It is not that democracy was at fault. After all, civil war has not become chronic on these shores, as it has in some nations where politics of force is the rule. One can at least say that the Civil War was exceptional; that may be the best thing that can be said about it. A fuller measure of applied democracy – e.g., a less precipitate casting of the die, a delay of secession till all the South could have taken part in a widely representative gathering, with the main issue reserved for popular vote – would probably have prevented the war. (In the secession movement of 1850 the more deliberate and coöperative method was used in the Nashville convention, and disunion was averted.) A better democratic expression – e. g., as to war department administration or exchange of prisoners – might have mitigated the war's abuses. To overlook many decades of peaceful development and take the Civil War as the exhibition of what American democracy does, would be to give an unfair appraisal. Nor does this probing of blunders involve lack of respect for the human beings of that generation. As individuals we love and admire them, these men and women who look at us from the tintypes and Brady photographs of the sixties, though we may have "malice toward some." The distortions and errors of the time were rather a matter of mass thinking, of unreasoning obsessions, of social solidification, and of politics.

3

In the present vogue of psychiatry, individual mental processes and behavior have been elaborately studied. Psychiatry for a nation, however, is still in embryo, though it is much the fashion to have discussions of mass behaviorism, public opinion, pressure groups, thought patterns, and propaganda. Writers in the field of history tend more and more to speak in terms of culture; this often is represented as a matter of cultural conflict, as of German against Slav, of Japanese against Chinese, and the like.[19] Scholars are doing their age a disservice if these factors of culture are carried over, as they often are, whether by historians or others, into justifications or "explanations" of war. The note of caution here should be a note of honest inquiry. If one talks of social forces they should be adequately understood. In the Nazi case, for example, it may be seriously doubted whether war arose from valid fundamental motives of culture or economics so much as from the lack of cultural restraint or economic inhibition upon militaristic megalomania. Modern wars have not relieved population pressures. In the days when Germany and Italy had African colonies the number of genuine, voluntary German and Italian settlers in those colonies was so small as to be practically negligible. Nor was Japan's population pressure appreciably relieved by the acquisition of Manchuria.

The idea that aggressive or imperialistic war is required in order to obtain raw materials is a colossal fallacy. A nation does not need to own or govern distant rubber producing or oil producing areas in order to have oil or rubber. As to "have not" nations, it is fallacious to apply that term to such a country as Germany in the Hitler days. Contemplating the tremendous munitions plants and factories of Germany and the manner in which raw materials were flowing in to support those plants, one could hardly say that Germany was a "have not" nation. Nothing is more fallaciously artificial than to suppose that a nation must make war and seize the areas from which its raw materials are to come. For how many countries would such a development be practically feasible? Of the more than sixty nations in the world of today, hardly more than one or two could actually seize and govern the raw material areas requisite for a whole nation's economy on the complex industrial pattern of present times. Hitler did not make war because Germany was actually being denied access to raw materials. War makers do not open up economic benefit so much as they stifle it. Their relation to culture is no better than their relation to economy.

There is the word *astrology* for bogus astronomy and *alchemy* for false chemistry. Ought there not be some such word for the economic alchemists of this world? Perhaps it exists in the word *autarchy*. Is it not in the category of bogus economics, or *ersatz* economics, that one should put those who present

[19] Concepts as to cultural conflict were presented at the meeting of the American Historical Association at Washington in December 1939. See "Educating Clio," *Amer. Hist. Rev.*, XLV, 505–532 (April 1940).

war as a matter of trade, supply, resources, needs, and production?

As for the Civil War the stretch and span of conscious economic motive was much smaller than the areas or classes of war involvement. Economic diversity offered as much motive for union, in order to have a well rounded nation, as for the kind of economic conflict suggested by secession. One fault of writers who associate war-making with economic advantage is false or defective economics; another is the historical fault. It is surprising how seldom the economic explanation of war has made its case historically – i.e., in terms of adequate historical evidence bearing upon those points and those minds where actually the plunge into war, or the drive toward war, occurred. Cultural and racial consciousness are as strong in Scandinavia or the Netherlands or Switzerland as in militarist-ridden countries. To make conquest a matter of culture is poor history. It may be the vanquished whose culture survives. Culture is not easily transplanted if force be the method. When war comes by the violence of a few in control and by the stifling of economic and cultural processes, it ill becomes the scholar to add his piping to the cacophonous blare of militaristic propaganda.

War causation tends to be "explained" in terms of great forces. Something elemental is supposed to be at work, be it nationalism, race conflict, or quest for economic advantage. With these forces predicated, the move toward war is alleged to be understandable, to be "explained," and therefore to be in some sense reasonable. Thought runs in biological channels and nations are conceived as organisms. Such thought is not confined to philosophers; it is the commonest of mental patterns. A cartoonist habitually draws a nation as a person. In this manner of thinking Germany does so and so; John Bull takes this or that course, and so on. When thought takes so homely a form it is hardly called a philosophical concept; on the level of solemn learning the very same thing would appear under a Greek derivative or Freudian label. However labeled, it may be questioned whether the concept is any better than a poor figure of speech, a defective metaphor which is misleading because it has a degree of truth.

Ruritania – to be no more specific – does so and so in the sense that it has a government, the government is presumed to act for the nation, and for political purposes there is no other way in which the country can act. The doubtful part is to infer that there is one directing mind for Ruritania which is the distillation of all the millions of minds. Where government has a bogus quality such an inference is more doubtful than if government is well grounded or soundly established. Given certain conditions of forced leadership and suppressed thought, the oneness of executive action in a nation may in fact represent nothing at all in terms of consolidated will and intent distilled from the whole mass. What passes for mass thought these days is not so much distilled as it is translated from golden plates handed down on some ideological Hill of Cumorah and read through the magic of authoritarian Urim and Thummim. The terrifying fact is that such bogus thought can be manufactured; it can be produced wholesale and distributed at top speed; it can control a nation; it is the shabby mental *ersatz* of an abnormal period.

War-making is too much dignified if it is told in terms of broad national urges, of great German motives, or of compelling Italian ambitions. When nations stumble into war, or when peoples rub their eyes and find they have been dragged into war, there is at some point a psychopathic case. Omit the element of abnormality, of bogus leadership, or inordinate ambition for conquest, and diagnosis fails. In the modern scene it fails also if one omits manipulation, dummies, bogeys, false fronts, provocative agents, fifth columns, made-up incidents, frustration of elemental impulses, negation of culture, propaganda that is false in intent, criminal usurpation, and terrorist violence.

4

There is no intention here to draw a comparison of the American Civil War with recent wars. The point is that sweeping generalizations as to "war causation" are often faulty and distorted, and that when such distortion is assisted by taking the Civil War as an alleged example, a word by the historian is appropriate. Unsound historical analogies may have present-day effects. The "explaining" of war is one of the most tricky of subjects. If the explanation is made to rest on the cultural or economic basis, it is not unlikely that the American war in the eighteen-sixties will be offered as a supposedly convincing example. The writer, however, doubts seriously whether a consensus of scholars who have competently studied that war would accept either the cultural or the economic motive as the effective cause.

If one were to explain, or record, the relation of this or that group or individual to the Civil War, he would have to recognize influences, situations, forces, or perhaps mere tricks of fate, that existed to a large extent outside the rational life of the particular group or individual. In such an inquiry he could rely on no one formula. He would have to make up a series of situations of which the following are only a few that might be mentioned: the despairing plunge, the unmotivated drift, the intruding dilemma, the blasted hope, the self-fulfilling prediction, the push-over, the twisted argument, the frustrated leader, the advocate of rule or ruin, and the reform-your-neighbor prophet.

Robert Toombs said he would resist Stephen A. Douglas though he could see "nothing but . . . defeat in the future";[20] there is your despairing plunge. Young Henry Watterson, then a Tennessee antislavery Unionist who fought for the Confederacy, is an example of the unmotivated drift. To many an individual the problem was not to fight with the side whose policies he approved of, but to be associated with the right set. Such an individual motive could not by a process of multiplication become in any reasonable sense a large-group motive. Yet it would be understandable for the individual. Usually in war time individuals have no effective choice of side, though in the American Civil War they sometimes did, especially on the border. Even where such choice was possible, the going to war by the individual in the sixties was due less to any broad "cause" or motive than to the fact that war existed, so that fighting was the thing to do. War participation is one thing; genuine and reasoned choice between war and peace, while that choice is open, is quite another.

The intruding dilemma was found in the broad border and the great upper South. The true interests and wishes of those regions did not determine the pattern that was set up before April of 1861. It was rather that, in a situation created

[20] Ulrich B. Phillips, ed., *The Correspondence of Robert Toombs, Alexander H. Stephens, and Howell Cobb*, in *Annual Report, 1911*, Amer. Hist. Assoc., II, 469.

by outside forces and thrust upon them, the people of Virginia, Kentucky, and neighboring areas were faced with two alternatives, both of which were utterly distasteful: either to fight against sister states of the lower South, or to join with those states in breaking the Union. The self-fulfilling prediction is recognized in the case of those who, having said that war must come, worked powerfully to make it come. The blasted hope – i.e., the wish for adjustment instead of butchery – was the experience of most of the people, especially in the border and upper South. The frustrated leader is seen in the Unionist who came to support secession, or in such Northerners as Thurlow Weed and William H. Seward who sought compromise and then supported war. The plea that "better terms" could be had out of the Union, implying a short, temporary secession gesture though uttered by determined secessionists, was the crafty argument used in enlisting Unionists for the cause of disunion. This might be dubbed the twisted argument. The push-over is seen in the whole strategy of secession leaders by which anti-secession states and Union-loving men were to be dragged in by the accelerated march of events.

These are things which belong as much to the "explanation" of the Civil War as any broad economic or cultural or elemental factor. It should be remembered how few of the active promoters of secession became leaders of the Confederacy; their place in the drama was in the first act, in the starting of trouble. The Rhetts and Yanceys were not the ones who steered the South through the bitter four-year crisis produced by secession. Nor should sectional preference cause one to forget how large a contribution to Union disaster, and how little to success, was given by Northern radicals during the war.

Clear thinking would require a distinction between causing the war and getting into it. Discussion which overlooks this becomes foggy indeed. It was small minorities that caused the war; then the regions and sections were drawn in. No one seems to have thought of letting the minorities or the original trouble makers fight it out. Yet writers who descant upon the "causation" of the war write grandly of vast sections, as if the fact of a section being dragged into the slaughter was the same as the interests of that section being consciously operative in its causation. Here lies one of the chief fallacies of them all.

Virginia would be an example to illustrate this point. Suppose one inquires into the "causes" of the Civil War. Suppose, then, he asks: Why did Virginians fight? Already he has shifted the discussion, perhaps without noticing it. In the period before Sumter Virginia avoided secession, having no important motive for leaving the Union. In fact, Virginia made a notable effort, through the Peace Convention, to preserve the Union, to keep things as they were, and to prevent war. The prevailing element in Virginia was not making a drive for secession and for a Southern Confederacy. The proceedings of the Richmond convention of 1861 proved that. Then events got out of hand. War broke out *for reasons outside Virginia*. The Old Dominion was *drawn into a war*, but as of early April 1861 it could not have been said that someone would have to begin a war in order for Virginian homes to be safe.

There was no prewar grievance, or Northern threat, or brutal aggression, that made the Union culturally, economically, or politically unendurable, or continued peace intolerable, to Virginia.[21] There was no controlling belief that an outside power was oppressing Virginia, and that war was required to throw it off. As for helping sister states, Virginia was willing to help them stay in the Union. Yet, war having been launched, men and women of Virginia verily believed that their homes and their true interests were at stake, though some of them, who had been strong Unionists, supported the Confederacy because in their view they could not loyally do otherwise once their state government had acted. While Virginia is presented as an example, the principle could be much more broadly applied. If the question before us is that of causing a war, one should speak to the point of causation. He merely clouds the issue if he confuses causation with those motives, sentiments, loyalties, unwelcome dilemmas, and necessities as to governmental adherence which exist in a given region after war has been launched, when the clock has passed the hour of causation or prevention, and when the practical question is that of participation.

5

In writing of human nature in politics Graham Wallas has shown the potent effect of irrational attitudes.[22] He might have found many a Civil War example. Traditional "explanations" of the war fail to make sense when fully analyzed. The war has been "explained" by the choice of a Republican president, by grievances, by sectional economics, by the cultural wish for Southern independence, by slavery, or by events at Sumter. But these explanations crack when carefully examined. The election of Lincoln fell so far short of swinging Southern sentiment against the Union that secessionists were still unwilling to trust their case to an all-Southern convention or to coöperation among Southern states. In every election from 1840 to 1852 Lincoln voted for the same candidate for whom many thousands of Southerners voted. Lincoln deplored the demise of the Whig party and would have been only too glad to have voted in 1856 for another Harrison, for another Taylor, or for Fillmore in the old Whig sense. Alexander H. Stephens stated that secessionists did not desire redress of grievances and would obstruct such redress. Prophets of sectional economics left many a Southerner unconvinced; it is doubtful how far their arguments extended beyond the sizzling pages of *DeBow's Review* and the agenda of Southern commercial congresses. The tariff was a potential future annoyance rather than an acute grievance in 1860. What existed then was largely a Southern tariff law. Practically all tariffs are one-sided. Sectional tariffs in other periods have existed without producing war. Such a thing as a Southern drive for independence on cultural lines is probably more of a modern thesis than a contemporary motive of sufficient force to have carried the South out of the Union on any broadly representative or all-Southern basis.

It must be remembered that the secession movement of 1860–61 proceeded, not by coöperative action of various states joining to deliberate and choose, as a group, between secession and union. It proceeded by separate state action, which was much easier for secession leaders to manage. Not even by separate state action was the upper South drawn

[21] "They say Virginia 'has no grievance . . . .' " Mary B. Chesnut, *A Diary from Dixie*, 50 (May 9, 1861).

[22] Graham Wallas, *Human Nature in Politics*, *passim.*

in until after the formation of the Confederacy and the beginning of war. Robert Barnwell Rhett, father of secession, was distrustful of coöperative action, or of anything like an all-Southern gathering to ponder the merits of secession. If modern writers have discovered a dominant movement over a wide region strong enough to have broken the Union for cultural reasons, they have found something which the promoters of secession did not know was there. Cultural factors are important; they should be studied for what they were, not cramped into a twisted or artificial formula or thesis.

It was hard for Southerners to accept the victory of a sectional party in 1860, but it was no part of the Republican program to smash slavery in the South, nor did the territorial aspect of slavery mean much politically beyond agitation. Southerners cared little about taking slaves into the territories; Republicans cared so little in the opposite sense that they avoided prohibiting slavery in territorial laws passed in February and March of 1861.[23]

Things said of "the South" often failed to apply to Southerners, or of "the North" to Northerners. "The North" in the militant prewar sense was largely an abstraction. To mention "Southern rights" as a generalization was easier than to analyze what the term meant. The Sumter affair was not a cause, but an incident resulting from pre-existing governmental deadlock. Sumter requires explanation, and that explanation carries one back into all the other alleged factors. In contemporary Southern comments on Lincoln's course at Sumter one finds not harmony but a jangling of discordant voices. Virginia resented Lincoln's action at Sumter for a reason opposite to that of South Carolina. Virginia wanted to preserve the Union; her resentment was in the anti-secessionist sense. By no means did all "the North" agree with Lincoln's course as to Sumter. Had Lincoln evacuated Sumter without an expedition, he would have been supported by five and a half of seven cabinet members, Chase taking a halfway stand and Blair alone taking a positive stand for an expedition.[24] What Lincoln refused as to Sumter was what the United States government had permitted in general as to forts and arsenals in the South. Stronger action than at Sumter was taken by Lincoln at Pickens without Southern fireworks. Search as one will, he simply cannot find an aggressive North bound up in the Sumter episode. Lincoln hoped the men in authority would realize that. There is no North-versus-South pattern that covers the subject of the forts. Nor can the war itself be adequately explained by the glib repetition of North-versus-South terms. These terms are usually excessive in what they purport to signify. Instead of denoting proved reality, phrases of this nature — "the North" wanted this; "the South" demanded that, etc. — should be regarded as a kind of stereotyped vocabulary.

Let one take all the factors traditionally presented — the Sumter maneuver, the election of Lincoln, abolitionism, slavery in Kansas, prewar objections to the Union, cultural and economic differences, etc. — and it will be seen that only by a kind of false display could any of these issues, or all of them together, be said to have caused the war if one admits the elements of emotional unreason and over-bold leadership. If one word or

23 These matters are treated by the writer in "The Civil War Restudied," *Journal of Southern History*, VI, 439–457 (1940).

24 Cabinet opinion on Sumter is here treated as of March 15, 1861. Two weeks later there was a somewhat different cabinet alignment.

phrase were selected to account for the war, that word would not be slavery, or economic grievance, or state rights, or diverse civilizations. It would have to be such a word as fanaticism (on both sides), misunderstanding, misrepresentation, or perhaps politics. To Graham Wallas misrepresentation and the coarser type of politics are the same thing.

The fundamental or the elemental is often no better than a philosophical will o' the wisp. Why do adventitious things, or glaringly abnormal things, have to be elementally or cosmically accounted for? If, without proving his point, the scholar makes war a thing of "inevitable" economic conflict, or cultural expression, or *Lebensraum*,[25] his generalizations are caught up by others, for it would seem that those historians who do the most generalizing, if they combine effective writing with it, are the ones most often quoted. Sometimes an author's pronouncements are taken as statements of laws whether he means them so or not; he is quoted by sociologists, psychologists, behaviorists, misbehaviorists, propagandists, and what not. When history is distorted it becomes a contributor to those "dynamic" masses of ideas, or ideologies, which are among the sorriest plagues of the present age.

[25] *Lebensraum* as a motive for producing a war is meaningless unless one links it with the following factors: the demand of an aggressive nation to own and rule where its nationals live; repudiation of the idea that Dutch can live with Swiss (to take a non-provocative example) except under Dutch domination; denial of *Lebensraum* to rudely dispossessed people even in their own country; and the sordid ideological justification of such denial on the ground that the intruding race with the bigger guns is superior by nature and has superior rights.

Bernard DeVoto:

SLAVERY AND THE CIVIL WAR

THIS is an appropriate time to talk about the Civil War, since Lincoln's birthday comes this month and since there is a new biography of him, Professor J. G. Randall's *Lincoln the President*. I wish somebody else would do this job, for it is going to be ungracious. I admire Mr. Randall's book, anyone who reads it must admire it, he has supplied me with many of my own historical ideas, and all of us will be appropriating parts of his new book without quotation marks from now on. But I want to discuss some ideas that are part of the book's frame of reference, ideas which have been proliferating among historians for a generation. They seem to me a regression, a deterioration which has reduced the validity of general ideas in American history.

Historians are mortal men. Also some historians tend to be timid about expressing judgments lest their colleagues deride them or prove them wrong, and some others hold themselves aloof from, or as they believe superior to, expressing judgments; these last feel that they are scientists working toward the establishment of fact, dealing passionlessly with inert data, without attitude toward them, outside the area where judgments, especially moral ones, can apply. Nevertheless, even the cagiest and the most detached acquire a body of historical judgment involuntarily. They absorb it from more forthright colleagues who believe that the essence of history is judgment. The intellectual climate of their time affects them. Fashions in thesis and dogma sift under their study doors. Historians who are now mature, the generation to which Mr. Randall belongs, happened to be young and impressionable at a time when an intellectual fashion was developing the (erroneous) thesis that the United States could and should have stayed out of the First World War and the (false) theorem that we were betrayed into it by propaganda. Furthermore, of that generation many who took up the study of the Civil War happened to be Southerners; that is, men who from their earliest childhood had been nourished on the most active of American social myths. Few if any of them have managed to work all the mythology out of their history.

This generation of historians has built up a body of judgment about the Civil War. Some of it is certainly sound, some certainly unsound. Some parts of it are not reconcilable with other parts, some parts cannot be reconciled with common sense or with experience. Some of its end-products in general idea have been proved untenable by the experience at

This article appeared as "The Easy Chair" in *Harper's Magazine*, 192 (February, 1946), 123–126.
Reprinted by permission of the publisher.

large of our generation. No historian, I suppose, accepts all of it, but every historian has incorporated a large or a small part of it into his thinking and assumes some of it as judgment on the way to forming further judgments. Let me call the body of judgment about the Civil War as a whole "revisionism." Well, revisionism, this historical generation's conclusions about the Civil War, contains much solid truth but it also contains some grave fallacies, some of which suggest an apt and accurate designation out of history, "doughface." My point is that, as a result of those fallacies, general ideas about the Civil War are less trustworthy today than they were a generation ago. There has been a regression in history.

I can state here only a few theorems from this body of judgment. The basic one holds that the Civil War was avoidable: that the moral, economic, social, political, and constitutional crisis could have been resolved short of war and within the framework of our institutions. Corollaries follow: that it should have been resolved and that therefore someone was to blame for the failure to resolve it. Who were the villains? A fundamental thesis of revisionism is that they were extremists, radicals, hotheads, agitators, manufacturers of inflammatory propaganda. It turns out that the decisive ones, so to speak the operative ones, were Northerners: abolitionists, freesoilers, the Republican Party, more radical reformers, in short, everyone who thought that the slavery issue was in some degree a moral issue. One of the most influential statements of this thesis is Professor Avery Craven's book, *The Coming of the Civil War.* I have been told that its title in manuscript was *The North's Mistake,* and that puts the idea into three words. An accessory theorem makes Stephen A. Douglas the tragic hero of the revisionists. His ideas ought to have prevailed: that they did not, which is the heart of our national tragedy, was due to the Republican or abolitionist agitation, which led the American people down a fatal path in pursuit of an unreal, a falsely represented, issue. In sequence, another theorem holds that, after Douglas had been repudiated, further Northern mistakes (procured by the radical Republican conspiracy) prevented a compromise which would have brought about a peaceful solution. *A posteriori,* it was the duty of the constitutionally elected (Republican) government of 1861 to abandon the constitutional structure and extemporize a new one which would contain the crisis – incidentally containing secession.

This is by no means all the revisionist body of judgment and, as I have said, probably no historian accepts all these theses, even as a system. But they have warped a lot of thinking, including some of Mr. Randall's. Now the Civil War is the crux of our history. You cannot set out to understand any part of our past, from the convening of the Constitutional Convention down to this morning, without eventually arriving at the Civil War. A few of the innumerable matters it involved were these: the successful functioning of constitutional government, the basic paradox and conflict in our social system, the basic conflict in our economy, the basic conflict and evasion in our political system. Whether or not the war was inevitable, the crisis was: these conflicts and paradoxes created problems which had to be solved. That they were not solved short of war is our greatest national tragedy. Our failure to solve them short of war is our greatest failure. The inescapable duty of historians is to explain that failure. But revisionist dogmas are carrying them farther from an explanation year by year.

Already those dogmas have made all but impossible the necessary first step, an accurate definition of the crisis. Take one which Mr. Randall accepts. The political conflict between the slave states and the free states entered a critical phase as soon as the invasion of Mexico made it clear that the United States was going to acquire an enormous new area by conquest. This area, which would be a national possession, would have to be organized as territories on the way to statehood. The prospect of so organizing it posed the question whether slavery should be legalized in it. This in turn forced consideration of a question which had been compromised, or settled, or evaded (depending on the point of view): whether slavery should be legalized in certain territories which were about to be organized in an area that was not part of the conquest. From that point on our central political, social, economic, and constitutional conflicts, all of which pivoted on slavery, were fought out on the question so posed, the status of slavery in the territories. So far as slavery was a cause of the Civil War or an issue of the conflict that ended in the war, it was nationally faced during the fifteen years before the war not primarily as slavery but as the question of slavery in the territories.

And that is a tragic fact. For it is clear to us today, and may have been half as clear to Americans North and South then as the revisionists say it was, that the economy of slavery could not possibly be adapted to or survive in the lands conquered from Mexico. And it is almost certain that slavery could not have been maintained in the territory of Nebraska and only a little less than certain that it could not have been maintained in the territory of Kansas, and these territories came to be the very vortex of strife. Therefore, according to revisionist dogma, the question of the legality of slavery in the territories was tangential, unreal, abstract, hypothetical, and almost immaterial. The pivotal strife in the fifteen tragic years that led to war resulted from the forcing of an unreal issue. Since the issue was forced by those who insisted on making the territories free soil (though why more by them than by those who insisted on making them slave is one of the more opaque portions of the revisionist gospel), the responsibility, after several lateral passes, must be charged to the Republican Party. Here, adopting the pure doughface doctrine, Mr. Randall looks on the men who stood by the central Republican demand, that slavery be forbidden in the territories, with a wild impatience. They were agitators; the best of them were bigoted or blind or misled, the worst of them corruptionists and disunionists. The principle on which they stood refusing to be moved was unreal, it had no existence. It was mere wind. They sowed it and the United States reaped the whirlwind.

But this is to miss the very essence of the national tragedy, and when history leads us off on this tangent it monstrously fails to explain our past. It is true that the question of slavery in the territories was a peripheral issue. But for historians and for those of us who try to learn from them *that is the point which must be explained.* It cannot be impatiently shrugged away or dismissed with a denunciation of some agitators whose blindness or wilfulness or bigotry is supposed to have dropped it in the path of men of good will and so switched them into the maelstrom.

Hold it to the light at a different angle. Slavery was at the very heart of our disequilibrium. It was the core of the social, the economic, the political, and the constitutional conflicts. But in the fifteen years left to the United States in which to face and solve the problem of slavery, the final decade and a half which ended in civil war, it did not face that problem but faced only a peripheral and even unreal issue that was ancillary to it. The federal powers and the state rights in regard to slavery, the future of slavery, the limitations of and on slavery, the constitutional questions of slavery, the relation of all these to the structure and functioning of our society — were fought out not in regard to themselves, the only way in which there was a possibility that they might be solved peacefully, but in regard to the status of slavery in the territories, where slavery could not exist. There, if you will, is a fact of illimitable importance. There is a fact which, if we are to understand ourselves, historians must explain.

To pass this off as an irresponsible mischief of politicians on the make is to go so far astray that history is forced entirely out of orientation and nothing less than a new beginning is required. What was there in the nature of the American people, in their institutions, in their development and way of life, or in the sum of all these and more, that prevented them from facing their inescapable problem squarely, in the nakedest light, with the soberest realism? What was there in the sum of American life that forbade us to go to fundamentals and forced us to escape through subterfuges into war? That is the question which historians must answer — the more necessarily, I submit, because in an answer to it there may be light or forecast, some judgment whether we are capable of squarely meeting the fundamentals of inescapable questions hereafter, perhaps even some wisdom that would help us to prepare to do so. But, because of the evolution of historical ideas which I have called revisionism, historians are farther from answering that question than their predecessors were a generation ago.

I do not venture to say why this regression has occurred. A friend of mine, whose hobby is the history of history, believes that in democracies historians have a tendency to romanticize defeated aristocracies. He points out that the English people, at the behest of their historians, especially the historians of this generation, are in a fair way to forget that they had a democratic revolution in the seventeenth century, that it settled basic problems for good and settled them in line with the development of the modern world, and that just because it did settle them Great Britain was able to maintain the domestic peace and exercise the world leadership that were hers during the two and a half centuries following it. It is certainly true that in English historiography today the picture of the roundheads who gave representative government to the English people has a striking likeness to that of the Republican malcontents and opportunists which our revisionists have been sketching. "In song and story," Mr. Randall remarks, "it is the South that has won the decision at Appomattox." Check. And one wonders if the South may not be winning the historiographic decision too — by evasion.

For the process of revisionism has developed a habit of understating certain things and passing quickly over others. That habit signalizes something to the inquiring mind; it looks like a repetition in the minds of historians of the evasion described above as a tragic failing of the American people, a repetition of fighting out the subterfuge instead of facing the fundamental reality. Thus the inquiring mind notes the agility with which revisionism dodges the question of minority dictation. A generation ago history clearly recognized that first the maintenance and then the loss of control of the national government by the slaveholding states, a minority, were important in the oncoming of the war. These facts have now been retired to the shadowy fringe. But there is a more central slurring-over which repeats the tragic evasion itself. In its concern to show that the Civil War was a product of hotheads, radical agitators, and their propaganda, an almost incidental result which could have been avoided if some extremists could have been induced to hold their tongues, history is in imminent danger of forgetting that slavery had anything whatever to do with the war. The revisionist gospel finds little time, and seems to have little inclination, to discuss whether in trying to understand the war we should take account of slavery as a social anachronism in the nineteenth century and as an obsolescent or even obsolete economy. It evades raising the question whether the Civil War had any of the quality that made the Glorious Revolution a struggle between the past and the future, whether it involved issues that were part of the movement of world society. As for considering even theoretically that the problem of slavery may have involved moral questions, God forbid. History will not put itself in the position of saying that any thesis may have been wrong, any cause evil, or any group of men heretical. A thesis may have been insufficient and a cause may have been defeated but, even at the end of the World War, history will not deal with moral values, though of course the Republican radicals were, well, culpable.

So, standing on this bulk of judgment, revisionism and Mr. Randall's book with it come to a crux of disorientation, a distorted perspective on what precipitated the war, secession. But if history cannot get secession into perspective, then it fails its job with the Civil War.

We have lately seen some younger historians whose specialty is the American Revolution come back forthrightly to the little red schoolhouse with a finding that, after all, the Revolution did have something to do with representative government, taxation without representation, and some of the things which the Declaration of Independence calls abuses of power. It is time to take a singularly radical, or reactionary, step and find some relation between slavery and secession on the one hand and the Civil War on the other.

Suggestions for Additional Reading

An indispensable introduction to the many historical writings about the Civil War is Howard K. Beale's excellent essay, "What Historians Have Said about the Causes of the Civil War," in *Theory and Practice in Historical Study: A Report of the Committee on Historiography* (Social Science Research Council, 1946), pp. 55–102. Appended to this essay is a most useful bibliography of writings dealing with the causes of the Civil War.

Good examples of emotional and partisan writing in the first generation after the Civil War are such works on the northern side as James G. Blaine, *Twenty Years of Congress* (Norwich, 1884–1886, 2 vols.); John A. Logan, *The Great Conspiracy: Its Origins and History* (New York, 1886); Henry Wilson, *History of the Rise and Fall of the Slave Power in America* (Boston, 1874–1877, 3 vols.). On the southern side a particularly vigorous attack on northern aggression is Edward Pollard's *Southern History of the Great Civil War in the United States* (New York, 1866).

The southern constitutional position is best presented in Alexander H. Stephens, *A Constitutional View of the Late War between the States. Its Causes, Character, Conduct and Results* (Philadelphia, 1868–1870, 2 vols.). A similar point of view is to be found in Jefferson Davis, *The Rise and Fall of the Confederate Government* (Richmond, 1881, 2 vols.). A notable attack on this states' rights position can be found in John W. Burgess, *The Civil War and the Constitution* (New York, 1901, 2 vols.). The relative importance of the states' rights issue is effectively analyzed in Arthur M. Schlesinger, *New Viewpoints in American History* (New York, 1922), pp. 220–243.

The importance of slavery in bringing on the conflict is emphasized in such classic works as James F. Rhodes, *History of the United States from the Compromise of 1850* (New York, 1900–1919), especially volumes 1–5; James Schouler, *History of the United States under the Constitution* (Washington, 1882–1894), especially volumes 4–6; and Hermann E. von Holst, *The Constitutional and Political History of the United States* (Chicago, 1877–1892, 8 vols.). The same emphasis is found in such shorter works as Albert Bushnell Hart, *Slavery and Abolition* (New York, 1906); Theodore C. Smith, *Parties and Slavery* (New York, 1906); and Jesse Macy, *The Anti-Slavery Crusade* (New Haven, 1919). Two recent works which shed more light on the influence of the abolition movement are Gilbert Barnes, *The Anti-Slavery Impulse* (New York, 1933), and Arthur Y. Lloyd, *The Slavery Controversy, 1831–1860* (Chapel Hill, North Carolina, 1939).

The Beards are probably the best-known exponents of an economic interpretation of the causes of the Civil War. For a similar point of view see Fred A. Shannon, *America's Economic Growth* (New York, 1940). An early economic interpretation was developed by Algie M. Simons in his *Social Forces in American History* (New York, 1911). In the same tradition is Louis M. Hacker, "The

American Civil War: Economic Aspects," *Marxist Quarterly* (April–June, 1937), pp. 191–213.

The main attack upon the economic interpretation has been made in recent years by the "repressible conflict" historians. J. G. Randall has kept up a ceaseless battle against the attempt to explain the cause of the Civil War in terms of the sectional economic differences in his *Civil War and Reconstruction* (Boston, 1937); "The Civil War Restudied," *Journal of Southern History*, 6 (November, 1940), 439–457; and *Lincoln the President* (New York, 1945, 2 vols.). Also worth reading in this connection are two books by Avery O. Craven, *The Repressible Conflict* (Baton Rouge, Louisiana, 1939) and *The Coming of the Civil War* (New York, 1942).

The importance of southern nationalism was suggested by Edward Channing in his *History of the United States* (New York, 1926), the sixth volume of which is entitled "The War for Southern Independence." A more detailed study of this cultural nationalism was made by Jesse T. Carpenter, *The South as a Conscious Minority* (New York, 1930). Nathaniel W. Stephenson's article, "Southern Nationalism in South Carolina in 1851," *American Historical Review*, 36 (January, 1931), 314–335, is also useful. A recent book which analyzes the politics of the fifties in relation to the whole cultural complex of divisive forces in American society is Roy F. Nichols, *The Disruption of American Democracy* (New York, 1948).